Family and Community Functioning

A Manual of Measurement for Social Work Practice and Policy

by
Ludwig L. Geismar

The Scarecrow Press, Inc.
Metuchen, N. J.   1971

Acknowledgments

Social science endeavors seldom spring full-blown from un-tilled soil. Typically they are preceded by and build upon the work of many others who have given thought to the same problem. This is particularly true of the effort before us. The instrument measuring family functioning which is described here is actually a revised version of one of the research products of the Family Centered Project of St. Paul, a pioneer undertaking dating back to the late 1940's whose goal was to serve what came to be known as the multi-problem family. The present work is based on my collaboration in the Family Centered Project with Beverly Ayres, whose premature death deprived the field of social work of an exceedingly able researcher.

I am most grateful to Charles J. Birt, former Director of the Family Centered Project and the United Fund and Councils of St. Paul, Minnesota, for permission to reproduce sections of the earlier manual entitled Measuring Family Functioning.

To Professor Ursula Gerhart of Rutgers University and formerly Associate Director of the Family Life Improvement Project I am particularly indebted. She assisted greatly in the development of the Community Functioning Scale and the instrument for the Self-Evaluation of Family Functioning. Professor Gerhart also took charge of the field work in which these tools underwent their first test, and of the family functioning coding operation which led to improvements in measurement procedure.

A special vote of thanks goes to Mrs. Harriet Fink, Research Associate in the Family Life Improvement Project, for doing the computer work required by this study and for assisting most ably in coding and other aspects of data analysis. To the conscientious and dedicated coding team, composed of Mrs. Fink, Mrs. Judy Schwartz, Mrs. Zona Fishkin, Mrs. Patricia Lagay, and Mrs. Dorothy Jaker, my hearty thanks. Special recognition is due to Professor Isabel Wolock, Assistant Director of the Rutgers Social Work Research Center, and to Bruce Lagay, formerly Assistant Director of the Family Life Improvement Project, for aiding this effort in innumerable ways. I am furthermore indebted to my Methods in Social Work research class of 1969, fall semester, for subjecting the Community Functioning Scale to a reliability test-retest and a field test in the community. Thanks also go to Professor Dingley and his students in the Community Organization class of the summer, 1970, for participating in the test-retest.

I owe a debt of gratitude to the U.S. Social Rehabilitation Service for its support of the Family Life Improvement Project (HEW Grant Number 190) from which some of that data were taken. I am also indebted to the Rutgers University Research Council for a faculty fellowship which allowed me to devote time to writing and to Dean Werner Boehm and the Rutgers Graduate School of Social Work for temporarily freeing me from teaching responsibilities and giving encouragement in these and related efforts.

I am grateful to Miss Bessie Vasiliou for helpful secretarial assistance and to Mrs. Anne Gill for a conscientious typing of the manuscript.

Finally, very special thanks go to my wife Shirley for extensive and creative editorial assistance.

Contents

Charts

I. INTRODUCTION

The juxtaposition of family and community in a manual on measurement may seem strange at first glance since the two concepts represent social systems which differ widely in size, life span, internal variability, purpose, goals, and a variety of other dimensions. Even sociological theorists, forever eager to build on common theoretical foundations, have found it necessary to start their theorizing about family and community from different vantage points. Why should anyone insist, then, on covering such diverse subject matter within the limited space of a small volume?

The answer lies outside the context of conceptual similarity. It derives mainly from the need of social work practice to address itself simultaneously or in close succession to the performance, problems, practices, and policies of both family and community. This dual focus in practice requires a parallel approach in research, if research is to play an effective part in the solution of problems encountered in the field.

The reciprocal relationship between family and community is well illustrated in the controversy that raged during the mid-sixties over the use of the concept multi-problem family. Responding to a flood of speeches and articles describing the characteristics of the multi-problem family, a number of writers, concerned with the functioning of the welfare system, pointed to its serious shortcomings and the reciprocal relationship between family and community problems. They believed, in effect, that the term multi-problem agency or community better characterized the problem situation than the concept multi-problem family.

While the nature of the foregoing controversy represents a polemic that cannot be resolved by logical means, there are, nonetheless, some basic truths contained in the argument that community and family problems are interdependent. The relationships

7

between disease and absence of medical service, or between
poverty and lack of employment or financial aid programs, have
been well documented. In a similar vein, the individual histories
of multi-problem families generally reveal a pattern of agency
failure to provide adequate and continuing service to those who cannot make it on their own.

The emergence and development of sub-disciplines--variously
referred to as practice methods or areas of concentration--within
American social work reveals a shifting of concern from micro-
systems such as the individual and the family to macro-systems
such as the state and national welfare systems. Social casework,
the first practice method to emerge as a full-fledged professional
discipline, has increasingly advocated that its service focus be extended from the individual to the nuclear family to kinship and
neighborhood groupings. Group work, community organization, and
social policy--the social work sub-disciplines that emerged in the
wake of social casework--broadened their intervention foci to suc-
cessively larger social systems. Their development within the
framework of the same profession provides testimony of a belief
shared by professionals that the interrelatedness of conditions,
behavior, functioning, problems, needs, and wants calls for a join-
ing of efforts in dealing with all of them.

Such cooperation tends to occur either at a high theoretical
level, in the formulation of educational programs, or at the
empirical level, in social work practice where services may need
to be coordinated in order to reach given objectives. Attempts to
relate problems of practice from two or more areas on intervention
by means of joint assessment, conceptualization, measurement, and
programming are relatively rare in the field of social work. Yet,
joint approaches aimed at determining the interrelationship of conditions, problems, and practices are the key to the growth of a
unified, science-based profession.

The present monograph seeks to initiate efforts to integrate
practice at the family and community levels by way of assessing
patterns of social functioning, seeing conceptualization and

measurement as first, but necessary, steps in attaining the more ambitious goals outlined above.

This manual is written mainly as a how-to-do-it book for the research practitioner. A discussion of the theoretical under-pinnings of measurement precedes the presentation of instruments and their use. For the sake of compactness, reliability and validity studies and other methodological endeavors, such as there are, are cited but not presented in full. The interested reader is encouraged to refer to the sources for a fuller treatment of each respective subject.

The family functioning scale is a modified version of that presented about a decade ago as part of the St. Paul Family Centered Project, while the community functioning scale represents the fruits of more recent efforts by the author. Neither instrument is presented as the last word in its respective kind of measure-ment. To the contrary, one is an instrument in transition, while the other is an early product of a one-year research effort. Like tools of measurement in the social and behavioral sciences in general, these scales should be used with discretion. They are presented as efforts which denote a systematized approach to the subject and which hold promise for the collection of data which will be useful to the researcher and practitioner. A decision about the utility of the kind of data that will be gathered and cor-related must be made by the potential investigator. The instru-ments will be found useful by some, irrelevant by others, and not quite suitable by still others. That third group of researchers might consider instrument modification as a solution to their re-search problems. Whichever road is decided upon, this writer hopes that the present volume will stimulate efforts toward a co-ordinated practice, guided by the collection of meaningful and valid family and community welfare data.

II. THE NEED FOR STANDARDIZED EVALUATION

During the 1950's the social work periodical literature
featured frequent articles exhorting administrators and researchers
to abandon ad hoc and intuitive approaches to the evaluation of
practice and to substitute instead efforts at objective, systematic
assessment. In the 1960's, as a result of a growing belief that
the scientific component needed strengthening, and also in
response to the prodding of granting agencies (especially those
fighting the War on Poverty), efforts at systematic evaluation
were greatly stepped up and published studies tended to replace
exhortations. A symposium, planned for January 1971 and sponsored by the Fordham University School of Social Services, was
set up to review the findings of studies on the effectiveness of
professional intervention in social work. It was able to identify
at least fifteen well planned and well executed projects, as well
as dozens of others which, in one form or another, fell short of
meeting minimum standards of scientific inquiry.

A national conference on family measurement, called in
Washington, D.C. in 1966 by the Welfare Administration (now
Social and Rehabilitation Service) of the U.S. Department of
Health, Education, and Welfare, identified the lack of adequate
instruments of measurement as a major reason for the dearth of
evaluative research.[1] The conference encouraged efforts to
develop appropriate research tools, calling this a necessary first
step in the evaluation of social services. This writer tends to
share the view expressed by the Washington conference, believing
that the number of far-reaching efforts, such as those registered
by the Fordham Symposium, would be much greater were this
shortage to be alleviated.

Although the number of practitioners who have to be sold
on the need for evaluation research is decreasing, there is still a

formidable amount of resistance or indifference to the idea.
While this writer cannot cite an exhaustive list of reasons for
this position, it is possible to identify a few major roadblocks.
Perhaps the main reason social welfare does not feel impelled to
evaluate its own product is that welfare agencies and institutions
enjoy a monopolistic position. [2]   They do not compete for clients.
The picture is, in fact, quite the opposite; social services are
very scarce and potential clients must assert themselves in order
to be accepted for treatment.   In public agencies complex bureaucratic procedures, preceding the actual service and discouraging
their use, are the norm.   Private agencies limit admissions with
the aid of a waiting list.   Survival and growth of the organization
do not depend greatly on the quality of the service rendered. As a
rule, accrediting and evaluation procedures by professional and
sponsoring bodies are not rigorous and provide no test of the
agency's effectiveness.

Consequently, social agencies feel little need to evaluate
their services scientifically.   Vis-à-vis this situation, it may be
asked why service organizations should even bother to invest in
improved assessment procedures.   The answer lies partly in the
realm of professional ethics, which makes it incumbent upon a
social welfare organization to use the most honest, systematic,
and objective methods of evaluating its work.   The other part of
the answer lies with the growing need for and mounting cost of
services, giving rise to pressures which call for a competent
evaluation of social welfare programs.

A second reason for the profession's failure to employ
standardized evaluation procedures is the expensive and time-
consuming character of such research.   Both are undeniably characteristics of social scientific evaluation methods, but both time
and cost have to be judged in relation to the total investment in
services.   In the absence of adequate evaluation, there is a great
likelihood that services may be quite ineffective and represent a
far greater cost to the community than the most extensive scientific
inquiry.

There is a third factor blocking or retarding efforts at evaluation. This is the credo, widespread among social helping practitioners, psychiatrists, clinical psychologists, social workers, educational and vocational counselors, and others, that the scientific procedure is not appropriate to their respective fields. This view may represent an honest, intellectual conviction, defensiveness about a service that contains weak spots, or a combination of the two. Formulating an answer to the cognitive position is well beyond the realm of this manual. On the more pragmatic side it is possible to point to numerous studies done in recent years in such areas as pre-school education, mental retardation, behavior therapy, etc., and to show how these have contributed to the constructive growth of practice.

Referring back to the question of cost and the time required for evaluation procedures, it must be stressed that both can be reduced by stages as the initial expensive efforts at instrument construction and standardization pave the way for studies, both large and small, which utilize the new products. However, a real change in the use of evaluation research by the helping professions will probably not take place until administrators and practitioners come to accept scientific evaluation as a standard component of practice.

III. FAMILY AND COMMUNITY FUNCTIONING: SOME COMMON DENOMINATORS AND DIFFERENCES

The Social Work Curriculum Study of 1959 defined the goals of social work as "... the enhancement of social functioning wherever the need for such enhancement is either socially or individually perceived."[1] Social functioning is a unifying concept by which human behavior can be viewed meaningfully within the context of the environment in regard to such criteria as stability, change over time, normalcy, adequacy, problemicity, and others.[2] The use of the concept social functioning as against such concepts as adjustment and adaptation denotes an important shift in social work from the study of properties of given objects to the study of relationships among parts of a system or among disparate systems. This shift parallels a similar change in focus in the biological and social sciences which occurred earlier in the century. Function, according to Blaine Mercer, may be defined as "the processes associated with the structure, or, more specifically, those contributions of a part to the continuity and ordered change of the larger whole to which it belongs."[3] The concept of social functioning has the advantage of being applicable to persons as well as to social systems, and of being definable in terms of social roles that are relevant to the many-faceted social work profession.

The application of the concept social functioning has been confined mainly to the study and treatment of individuals and families. Few efforts have been made to extend the concept to such larger social systems as agency, institution, neighborhood, and community, which are also the concerns of the profession. Such an extension calls for an identification of common denominators inherent in the concept's use in relation to specific subject matter, such as economic functioning, health functioning, welfare functioning, etc. Since the concern of the present manual covers family and community, the discussion here will be confined to these two systems.

13

Functioning, as stated above, denotes a process in which the action of the parts of a system are viewed in relation to their contribution toward its continuity. Within the context of social work, continuity can be defined more normatively as behavior connected with the goals or values of autonomy, integration, and viability of the system. [4] Autonomy means existence as a separate entity, the maintenance of a measure of independence, control over the component parts of the system, and the existence of a positive image of self, supported by the use of symbols which are characteristic of the system. Integration denotes interaction that serves to unify and harmonize the constituent elements of the system and fosters interdependence which furthers its instrumental and expressive goals. Viability can be defined as a capacity to confront problems[5] and to survive under adverse conditions. Stability as well as a capacity for ordered change are characteristics of viability. Autonomy, integration, and viability are abstract concepts which need translating into measurable indicants that are completely relevant to the purposes of the study.

The social work focus of the present endeavor dictates a welfare concern in the broadest sense, by which is meant a consideration of the material, biological, social, and emotional well-being of the individuals composing the system. Individuals may be said to constitute the major constituent parts of the nuclear family--except for such subsidiary systems as parents and siblings that may on occasion also receive primary emphasis in family research. In the community, by contrast, individuals represent the beginning link in a chain of systems which vary in size, complexity, length of tenure, and other characteristics. Most students of the family are concerned with such properties of the individual as personality, marital satisfaction, sexuality, social roles, power, and child-rearing practices. To be sure, interactional analysis deals with the variables of sub-systems, but such analysis uses the individual as an immediate referent. The study of the community, on the other hand, might be conducted at levels where individual behavior is only of secondary importance as compared

with the collective properties of given entities or systems.   For
instance, a study of industrialization may deal mainly with changes
in production, consumption, employment patterns, and the growth
of unions, or research on mobility may concern itself with the
social, ethnic, and religious composition of census tracts or
neighborhoods.

The study of community functioning from the point of view
of the welfare of its citizens represents only one of several research foci, without any assumption that the study of the individual
is the ultimate or most significant perspective in community analysis. [6] The choice of focus in this project stems from a theoretical
orientation whose immediate goal is service to maximize the well-
being of the individual and the family.   It is this orientation which
guides the selection of criteria for the study of social functioning.

Given the general systems goal dimensions of autonomy,
integration, and viability, we need to determine their significance
relative to family and community needs.   The welfare and service
focus of the endeavor decrees an emphasis on the integrative aspects of the system over autonomy and viability.   Since we judge
the system's effectiveness chiefly in terms of the well-being of its
members, our concern is more with the way these are being served
than with the system's ability to act independently and to cope with
diverse problems, even though these may in the long run affect the
integrative goals of the system.

At the family level the integrative goal function is manifest
in the family's performance of tasks such as providing security,
love, social and intellectual stimulation, and meeting some instrumental needs.   Autonomy is inherent in the family's ability to act
as a provider--within the limits of the prevailing norms--and to create
a sense of family solidarity.   Viability resides in the family's
capacity to overcome social, emotional, and economic crises and
meet economic needs.

At the level of the community, the integrative goal covers
the provision of services and resources for income, employment,
housing, social security, health, social adjustment, and

socialization. Viability pertains to the social control function of
maintaining order, giving legal and physical protection, and enforc-
ing a degree of conformity with community norms. Autonomy,
though important in the realm of policy making, is only indirectly
measurable at the level of citizens' behavior in the degree to which
community members are able, through political and administrative
processes, to determine community policy. Autonomy is also
reflected in the degree to which the community is able to meet
its citizens' instrumental needs. In short, from the perspective
of community members in general, the assessment of community
functioning revolves mainly around the integrative aspects of the
system, while viability and autonomy either play a secondary role
or are not directly measurable.

This manual's basic approach to studying the social functioning of both family and community is to assess the way in which the
individual and collective needs of the members are being met. The
degree to which this does or does not happen becomes a criterion
for judging the functioning of the respective systems. The similarity in the philosophy of evaluating family and community, however, does not guarantee a similarity in methodology. The reasons for the differences in methodological approaches stem from
the nature of the relationship between the individual and the respective system.

Allowing for some exceptions, the individual and the family
interact with one another almost continuously and shape each other's
functioning and development. The family as a group is aware of
the roles of its members and is informed about their behavior,
attitudes, and values. Each family member in turn finds himself
responding much of the time to the family as a collectivity. Most
individuals find, however, that the community is not an entity with
which they interact all the time. The closeness of the relationship
between community and individual is conditioned, to be sure, by
many factors, such as the size, prestige, and power of the community, the status and length of residence of the individual, but
the average person finds that community membership is not as

compelling an association as family membership, and his functioning or that of his family is not so strongly influenced by the city,
town, or hamlet in which he lives.   The community, on its part,
is not aware--again allowing for some variation due to size and
the influence of the individual--of the resident per se but only of
groups of tax payers, commuters, shoppers, demonstrators, etc.

The nature of the foregoing relationships determines the
reciprocal expectations between individuals and the systems to
which they belong.   Such expectations are extensive between individual family members and the family as a system.   Each individual is expected to contribute according to his ability, and the
family as a whole is expected to meet many of the basic needs of
its members.   The reciprocal expectations between individual (or
family) and community are much more limited in scope.   Community residents must pay taxes, obey the laws and ordinances,
and conform, more or less, to local mores.   But the residents,
in turn, have certain expectations regarding the community's obligations toward them.   They generally feel entitled to educational
and welfare services, to roads, sewers, public transportation,
and other utilities either offered directly or through a concession-
aire given the community franchise.

Individuals and families are most likely to judge a community by the services it offers, and that judgment is selected
here as a basis for measuring community functioning.   Citizens'
assessment of services is a relatively universal and unambiguous
criterion, set in the very complex and infinitely variable pattern
of roles, relationships, and functions which characterizes communities.   The relationship of individuals to their families, by contrast,
is more direct and immediate, permitting ready investigation into
the several dimensions in which individuals and families relate to
one another and serve each other.   Relationships between individuals and families can be identified and evaluated within a framework of cultural norms and expectations.   Individual-community
relationships, however, are ill defined, except as they overstep
the wide boundaries of the law.   Without a clear definition they

cannot be assessed very readily relative to existing societal standards or norms. This vagueness is, in fact, largely responsible
for the lack of definite standards by which such relationships might
be judged.

Family and community functioning also suggest substantially
different assessment procedures for the collecting of data. When
studying the family each member becomes a potentially valid in-
formant regarding most aspects of family life, while family life as
a whole can be studied readily by means of observation, interviews,
tape recordings, questionnaires, and other techniques. In community research, however, the average community member has only
limited usefulness as a source of information since he has been
exposed to just a few aspects of community life, and the study
itself is so complex, time consuming, and expensive an endeavor
as to be beyond the reach of most investigators. Therefore, the
study of family functioning is likely to utilize a variety of data
collection techniques that capture many dimensions of family living,
while research on community functioning, in avoiding the danger of
becoming bogged down in the complexity of data, is prone to make
use of a relatively simple and standardized instrument, tapping the
most significant dimension for gathering information from residents.

Before discussing the specific approaches to the study of
family and community, their functional interrelationship within a
research framework deserves additional comment. Arensberg and
Kimball, in an essay on the evaluation of community study, [7] state
that "the community offers the most significant focus, the most
viable form of human groupings, for direct innovation, for massive
and continuous stimulation of cultural change. "[8] Whether one accepts the superlative formulation "most viable" or simply accepts
the proposition that the community is one important agent for innovation and cultural change, there would seem to be little doubt
that the community constitutes the immediate environment within
which individuals and families express themselves socially, culturally, and politically and where change and innovation are
registered in a tangible manner. In view of this, the study of

family which does not address itself fully to the community in which
the family resides, would seem to omit a research aspect that is
essential to a full understanding of its life.

The interrelationship between family and community would
seem to be particularly pronounced where social service is the
focus of research. Social services of one form or another are
probably rendered to all community residents. However, certain
segments of any population receive more services than others because of their dependence on community sponsored programs:
families with school-aged children, the unemployed or underem-
ployed, other categories of economically deprived, the sick and
the physically handicapped, the maladjusted and the mentally ill,
old people without financial means, deprived ethnic minorities, and
others. The greater the families' dependence on community resources, the greater the interaction between these families and
the community. The needs of a population affect the total character of the community, its goals, political processes, service
structure, self-image, etc. The kind of services, facilities, and
resources families get from the community--or in the community,
if it serves merely as a mediator and referral agent--tends to
have an impact upon the functioning and development of these
families.

Students of the community have been inclined to look upon
the system as a function of such population factors as social class,
ethnicity, age groupings, migration patterns, suburbanization, etc.
Less common are efforts to inquire into the effects of the community upon its residents. The methodological problems inherent in
such investigations are considerable because they require longitudinal designs which permit a tracing of community influences on
matched populations, settling in one type of community or another.
An alternate possibility is offered by repeated cross-sectional
studies in which efforts are made to deduce the effects over time
of different community systems on comparable population groups.

Social welfare research affords a special opportunity to
study the influence of the community on the population by testing

the effects of community-wide measures on the incidence and prevalence of given community problems. The epidemiological approach,
widely employed in public health, is particularly suited for such
research. Programs to remedy, control, or prevent a given
problem are generally administered within a larger social service
context made up of existing resources, bureaucratic procedures,
attitudes of officials, etc. All of these are related to the way
programs are perceived and utilized by the population for which
they are intended, and they, in turn, are affected by the programs
themselves. Therefore, a study of the effects of programs and
services can be made particularly meaningful by including in the
design a measurement of the most relevant community variables.

The foregoing considerations have spurred the present
effort at developing tools that may help to bring into meaningful
juxtaposition certain aspects of community and family systems.
The common study concept chosen, as stated earlier, is social
functioning, and it was operationalized with reference to the needs,
problems, and aspirations of populations. This is a selective
focus especially attuned to service planning and operation. The
instruments that are presented here, like most tools of social
measurement, are instruments "in becoming" rather than finished
and final products. Researchers are encouraged to view them as
prototypes or models for ongoing endeavors and to make whatever
adaptations are required by the goals of their study.

The process of measuring family and community functioning is described in this volume under separate headings following
a discussion of the theoretical underpinnings of each approach.
We shall begin with family functioning, the more familiar of the
two concepts, and the one which provides the first span of the
complex bridge between the individual and the social environment
in which he lives.

IV.   MEASURING FAMILY FUNCTIONING

IV.   1.   Introduction

Service to families is not a new phenomenon in social work, for both the Settlement Movement and the early social casework school in America were oriented toward the family.   In the 1930's the focus in casework began to shift significantly toward the individual, partly as a result of the influence of Freudian psychology but also in response to the mushrooming public welfare programs which were assuming responsibility for service to families. This left the professional casework agencies free to treat the psycho-social problems of individuals.   In the 1950's professional social work once again directed its attention toward the family, an interest which was shared by segments of the psychiatric profession. [1]

The emphasis of this new movement was, as it should have been, on diagnosis and treatment.   The conceptualization underlying practice, though influenced by the social sciences and particularly sociological theory on the family, remained basically ad hoc and underdeveloped.   There were few efforts by the social work community to utilize practice in such a way as to test whatever theoretical propositions had been accepted by the practitioners.

If the practice-related family theory was not well developed, practice-focused measurement was practically nonexistent during the 1950's.   Kogan and Shyne, reporting on the development of the Community Service Society Movement Scale (Hunt-Kogan Scale), pointed out that initial efforts were directed toward rating the total case (usually a family) and that "this approach stemmed directly from the family-centered approach of the worker involved in the research program. "[2]   The effort at total case or family measurement was eventually abandoned in favor of measuring individual behavior, because of the difficulties workers experienced in

rating groups of individuals and because the change in family
composition (in follow-up studies) made it impossible to compare
before and after ratings. "Many workers, " Kogan and Shyne stated,
"also reported that they had to judge change in the individual before
they could render the judgment for the family. "[3]

The crux of the difficulty encountered by the researchers is
contained in the last statement. The failure to carry out family
measurement stemmed mainly from the fact that the family was
viewed as an aggregate of individuals rather than as a social system. If the family is conceptualized as a mere aggregate of persons, the absence or addition of one or more individuals poses a
major problem in repeated measurement. If, on the other hand,
the family is defined as a system, the turnover of family members
is of secondary importance as long as the group of family members
continues to operate as a system.

The measurement endeavor reported here is a revised version of the evaluative method that has come to be known as the
St. Paul Scale and was developed in the late 1950's in conjunction
with the Family Centered Project of St. Paul, Minnesota. [4] The
Scale was originally devised for evaluating the social functioning
of socially disorganized families, but it has more recently been
used in slightly revised form in research with normal families as
well. Differences in the application of the Scale to one type of
population or another will be dealt with following a discussion of
the instrument itself.

IV. 2. Theoretical Underpinnings

In the quest for a universal definition of the family, anthropologists and sociologists have been studying and comparing primitive and technologically advanced societies. [5] The extensive variations in structure and function pose problems for the scholar who is intent upon formulating definitions which are true common denominators. Our task of definition is made easier by the fact that our research is confined to families (mostly American) living in western cultures. In our study the family is structurally a group of two or more people, including at least one parent or parent substitute and one dependent child, related by blood, marriage, or adoption. The group is held together by moral, social, and legal rights and obligations, and carries out socially expected functions which include the socialization of children and the provision of love, security, food, clothing, and shelter for all its members.

The family is a system by virtue of the fact that its constituent parts interact and bear a definable relationship to one another. At one level, this system is composed of persons who reside together, talk to one another, express love or hate to each other, join in certain tasks, help or antagonize each other, engage in sexual intercourse, and communicate in other ways. At another level, the family is composed of many roles which are socially defined and stand in some complementary relationship to each other. The roles revolve around efforts to carry out functions leading to the attainment of family objectives which have been spelled out in part by society--these are mainly the legal and moral aspects of such goals--and in part by the family itself, with the aid of relatives, friends, and other reference groups.

By and large, the research effort is directed to the study of the nuclear family composed of parents and dependent children. On occasion the unit of study will deal with various types of extended family, perhaps including grandparents, relatives, children

of relatives, and other household members not related by blood.
Measurement will take account of these individuals to the extent
that they may be considered part of the family system, or, put
differently, to the extent that their roles mesh with the roles of
nuclear family members.

Following Bell and Vogel[6] and other writers whose names
are commonly identified with the structural-functional approach in
the study of the family, [7] a guiding proposition of the present
study is that an individual family is a social system, with functional requirements or prerequisites comparable to those of other
social systems.

There is some variation in the way scholars have defined
functional prerequisites of the family. Previously we listed
autonomy, integration, and viability as perhaps the most basic
goals of any social system. The systems themselves, as indicated earlier, differ with regard to the degree of importance
each of these goals assumes for the system's continuity. This
difference in emphasis determines the way in which functional
prerequisites are identified and defined. Moreover, different
scholars have conceptualized the function in dissimilar ways in
keeping with their own theoretical approaches to the subject.

William J. Goode lists reproduction, status placement,
biological maintenance, socialization, and sexual controls as functions classically assigned to the family. [8] Marion Levy identifies
role differentiation, allocation of solidarity, economic allocation,
political allocation, and allocation of integration and expression
as so-called "structural prerequisites" rather than functional prerequisites, because his points of reference are the sub-structures
that carry out the functions. [9] Kingsley Davis considers reproduction, placement, maintenance, and socialization as core functions of the family while other functions are viewed as by-products
of the primary functions. [10]

The social welfare focus of the present study suggests an
organization of functions relative to relationship patterns in the
family (intra-familial relationships), with persons outside the

family (extra-familial relationships), role behavior of individuals, and instrumental forms of behavior such as maintaining the home and providing for the economic and health needs of family members. The functions, to be identified in more detail below, reflect inter- action patterns, roles, and task performances among members of the family system and between members of that system and other surrounding systems such as work, school, social peer groups for children and adults, neighbors, health and welfare agencies, formal organizations for sociability and recreation, and others. The conceptualization and organization of functions are designed as an aid in family behavior according to culturally and profes- sionally prescribed norms and to facilitate programming for inter- vention, because the categorization denotes a grouping of behavior and situations that have their counterpart in the activities of the potential intervener, particularly the social worker.

The reader may be interested in learning how the scheme for categorizing family functions evolved, and a momentary de- parture from the discussion of the theoretical framework may be in order.   Work on the scheme known as the St. Paul Scale of Family Functioning has been characterized by an interweaving of both the empirical and the theoretical.   The Scale categories were derived from a social diagnostic study originally developed and used by a group of caseworkers in the Services to Families and Children Project sponsored jointly by the New York City Youth Board and the Department of Welfare.   The social diagnostic study was introduced to the Family Centered Project by Alice Overton, Project Director from 1955 to 1959 and formerly co- ordinator of the New York Project.

The Family Centered Project research team, composed of Beverly Ayres and myself, was charged with the development of an instrument for the assessment of movement in multi-problem families.   We held regular meetings with Project workers to ex- amine the adequacy of the diagnostic outline, reviewing first of all the category scheme for comprehensiveness of content and exclusiveness of classification--assuring the same content would

be included in only one category.   This review was based on existing case data which the social workers were discussing in their
weekly in-service training seminars.   Secondly, we checked the
existing classification scheme for the possible omission of content
which was included in the case material.   To do this we reviewed
other family classification systems as well as family case data
collected by other investigators in order to establish what family
roles, thought to be of importance for understanding and treating
families, were not covered by the original scheme.

A conspicuous example of omission was the category "social
activities. "   Its non-inclusion reflected a service orientation best
characterized as problem-focused, lacking concern with areas of
functioning generally free of serious crises.   The practitioners
responded positively to the suggestion that social activities be included among the social study categories, for it reinforced an already present conviction that effective service to families must
build upon strengths as well as weaknesses.

These empirically derived categories would have utility for
research only if they could be organized in a theory-relevant format
and operationalized for purposes of measurement.   The structure-
function approach to studying the family, as indicated above, furnished some important leads to organizing the data, for it led to
the identification of functions relative to the part they played in
assuring the continuity of the system, without incorporating the
equilibrium model or the teleological overtones of some of the
writers of the functionalist school. [11]

If measurement is the goal, the most basic procedure is to
define criteria by which family functioning can indeed be measured.
It must be emphasized that choosing the criteria is also the most
controversial of undertakings, since it forces the researcher to
play a nontraditional role--at least nontraditional for the bulk of
social researchers--by committing himself to a normative evaluation procedure.

"A precondition to an evaluation study, " Edward Suchman
wrote, "is the presence of some activity whose objectives are

assumed to have value. ... " He goes on to define value ". . . as any
aspect of a situation, event, or object that is invested with a preferential interest as being 'good,' 'bad,' 'desirable,' 'undesirable,' or
the like. "[12] Values are, of course, relevant to social services and
to the helping professions. As administrators, professionals, and
the public make decisions on the rendering of services, so they
also commit themselves, explicitly or implicitly, to the objectives
of these services. Since the services are generally rendered to
individuals or groups, the definition of objectives must be expressed
in terms of characteristics or qualities attached to the objects of
service. A listing of such characteristics or qualities in terms of
better or worse, more or less desirable, denotes a listing of values.

In designing social work services to families, goals need to
be formulated which bear a relationship to what it is in families
that is viewed as good or desirable. People will more readily
agree on the fundamentals of the good life, such as happiness,
health, and security, than on the specifics under this heading. It
is not altogether certain that a broad, common denominator or
desiderata can be formulated for any one society, let alone for all
of mankind. Nonetheless, and here is where the researcher has
to go out on a limb, evaluation study requires a pinning down of
factors by which an activity can be judged. The activity around
which present evaluation efforts revolve is professional social work.
Therefore, the social work practitioner who defines treatment goals
for families should be able to supply the most relevant list of
standards of functioning by which the effectiveness of services can
be judged.

The foregoing assumption guided the scale construction activity in the St. Paul Family Centered Project not only in relation
to choice of categories of functioning (see above) but also in the
selection of criteria for assessing the quality of family functioning.
Through a perusal of workers' statements on treatment goals for
families and with the aid of a social worker-researcher dialogue
aimed at clarifying service goals which were implied but not
enunciated, it was possible to evolve a composite measure for

evaluating family functioning. [13]   This measure comprises two broad
dimensions on which professional judgment is being made.   The
first we shall call the health-welfare dimension, and it concerns
the basic total well-being and happiness of family members.   The
second is the conformity-deviance dimension which determines the
extent to which family members as a group, sub-group, or as individuals are integrated into or are at odds with various social
systems, such as family, community, and society.

The health-welfare dimension includes two sub-areas which
deal with the following two questions: does behavior contribute or
is it harmful to the physical, social, and emotional well-being of
family members? and is a family member's behavior personally
satisfying and commensurate with his potential for social functioning?   The conformity-deviance dimension also is composed of two
sub-areas which address themselves to the following questions:
are laws observed or violated? and is behavior in harmony or in
conflict with the mores and standards of a community or a family's
status group?   These four sub-dimensions are to be viewed as
common denominators of criteria for evaluating functioning, and
they need to be specified further in relation to particular categories
of behavior.   For instance, with regard to the care of children,
the health-welfare dimension suggests that children should feel
loved, physically and socially secure, be adequately clothed and
fed, etc., while the conformity-deviancy dimension implies that
they should feel accepted by others, that their behavior should
not be outside the law or in violation of the norms of their parents
and peer groups, and so forth.

On the other hand, it needs to be stated that not all sub-
dimensions are equally applicable to all types of family functioning.
For some forms of behavior one kind of sub-area is likely to be
of far greater importance than the other.   For instance, in seeking
to determine the adequacy of a marital relationship, the question
of whether partners meet each other's emotional, sexual, and
social needs (health-welfare dimension) figures much more prominently than the issue of whether their relationship is a legal one or
is condoned by the community.

By identifying the dimensions for judging social functioning
we have only delineated the direction of evaluation. To complete
the process it is also necessary to define the limits of the dimensions which will determine whether functioning is held to be good
or bad, desirable or undesirable. The definition of limits, like
the identification of the dimensions, was accomplished by reviewing
the treatment plans of social workers and their decisions to close
cases because treatment goals were deemed to have been attained.
Additionally, however, the researchers found it necessary to review
both the casework literature and family and child welfare legislation in order to determine cut-off points of adequacy-inadequacy.
These boundaries were, in fact, a combination of legal and professional considerations. The former pertain mainly to behavior
officially stamped undesirable by the community or its delegated
representative and generally declared as a reason for intervention.
The latter concern professional judgment on what is and what is
not desirable, especially in areas where the law or local statutes
do not specify the limits of the allowable.

By and large, law and professional judgment supplement
each other. The limits of the law in the area of family and child
welfare are wide and leave much undefined territory. Professional
judgment seeks to operate within the limits of the law and to provide guidance in areas of behavior where the law supplies none.
Occasions arise, nonetheless, when the law and professional standards are in conflict. This occurs most commonly with regard to
archaic, or sometimes plainly unenlightened, legislation in the
area of conjugal relations, birth control, and the rights of low-
income tenants. In those instances, the decision on cut-off points
for rating family functioning was guided by professional rather than
legal standards.

Before presenting the criteria for rating family functioning,
the product of a one-year research effort, it may be helpful to
tie together in tabular form the chain of conceptual formulations
leading to an evaluation of family functioning.

Chart I shows the functional prerequisites of the family

CHART I.   CONCEPTUAL FRAMEWORK FOR RATING FAMILY FUNCTIONING

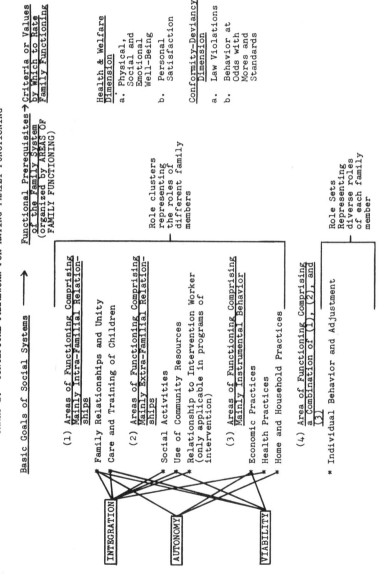

Basic Goals of Social Systems →

INTEGRATION
AUTONOMY
VIABILITY

(1) Areas of Functioning Comprising Mainly Intra-Familial Relation-ships

Family Relationships and Unity
Care and Training of Children

(2) Areas of Functioning Comprising Mainly Extra-Familial Relation-ships

Social Activities
Use of Community Resources
Relationship to Intervention Worker (only applicable in programs of intervention)

(3) Areas of Functioning Comprising Mainly Instrumental Behavior

Economic Practices
Health Practices
Home and Household Practices

(4) Area of Functioning Comprising a Combination of (1), (2), and (3)

* Individual Behavior and Adjustment

Functional Prerequisites → Criteria or Values
of the Family System   by Which to Rate
(organized by AREAS OF   Family Functioning
FAMILY FUNCTIONING)

Role clusters representing the roles of different family members

Role Sets Representing diverse roles of each family member

Health & Welfare Dimension
a. Physical, Social and Emotional Well-Being
b. Personal Satisfaction

Conformity-Deviancy Dimension
a. Law Violations
b. Behavior at Odds with Mores and Standards

organized in terms of nine areas of social functioning. As was pointed out previously, this special form of categorization was found suitable for relating family data to programs of social intervention. The category Relationship to Intervention Worker, in particular, is relevant to this focus of study and should be omitted where programs of services are not involved. The predominate frame of reference for the organization of categories are lower-class families. For that reason no attempt was made to detail political functioning, for instance, generally viewed as being characteristic of the upper middle class or of elite groups among the lower classes. Political functioning in our scheme is subsumed under the area Social Activities in general and the sub-area of Formal Associations.

Religious functioning is another example of a type of family behavior not given separate area coverage. Religious functioning is much more limited in scope among urban lower or working-class families than among the rural population or the urban middle class. Religious functioning in the above scheme is covered under the areas Social Activities (sub-category Formal Associations) and Use of Community Resources (sub-category Church or Religious Institutions). Any measurement undertaken with families in which political or religious functioning plays a prominent role should make provisions for a separate assessment of these two types of functioning.

An important conceptual distinction is to be noted among the nine areas of family functioning shown in Chart L Eight of these, all but Individual Behavior and Adjustment, denote areas of functioning where individual roles converge and cluster in order to accomplish given tasks, such as rearing children or keeping house. Individual Behavior and Adjustment, by contrast, signifies role sets of individuals defined as "the complex of positions in which an individual holds simultaneous membership."[14] It follows that an evaluation of Individual Behavior and Adjustment takes into account the way an individual functions in his diverse, socially assigned roles. The adult female in a family, for example, would

be rated by the way she performs her roles as wife, mother, homemaker, neighbor, member of the P. T. A. , etc.   Her male child
would be judged in terms of his performance as son, student, peer
group member, newspaper boy, and others.

     In rating the areas of functioning which represent clusters
of the roles of individual family members, our chief concern is
not with the individuals themselves but with the way in which the
tasks or functions are carried out.   In other words, in rating
Economic Practices we are interested in the way the functions of
providing an income and managing the money are performed.   The
functionaries, i. e. , those who earn the money and budget it, are
of secondary importance.   In assessing Individual Behavior and
Adjustment, on the other hand, each individual or functionary needs
to be rated, and that rating is based on the way he manages his
role set or performs the various roles assigned to him.   Chart II
provides a simplified example of the relationship between social
roles and individual behavior and functions.

     The next two sections, numbers 3 and 4, will detail the
procedure for collecting and presenting data on family functioning
in an organized form.   Section 5 gives a listing of criteria for
rating the content in each area and sub-area.   Subsequent steps
comprise instructions for rating the families' social functioning
and for statistical analysis.   A case study of a family is used to
illustrate the rating process in a more tangible fashion.

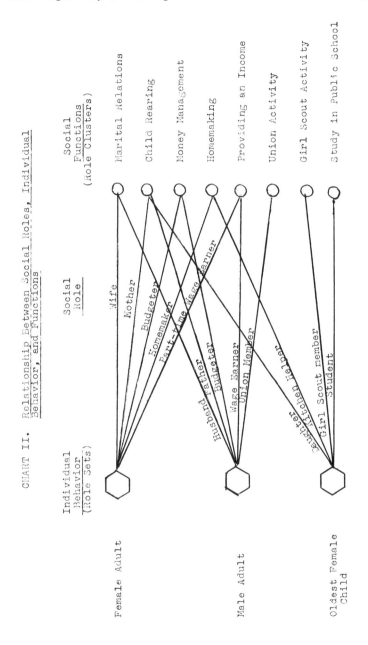

CHART II. Relationship Between Social Roles, Individual Behavior, and Functions

Individual Behavior (Role Sets)

Social Role

Social Functions (Role Clusters)

Female Adult

Wife
Mother
Budgeter
Homemaker
Part-time Wage Earner

Male Adult

Husband
Father
Budgeter
Wage Earner
Union Member

Oldest Female Child

Daughter
Kitchen Helper
Girl Scout member
Student

Marital Relations
Child Rearing
Money Management
Homemaking
Providing an Income
Union Activity
Girl Scout Activity
Study in Public School

IV. 3. Documenting the Families' Social Functioning

The decision to gather information with the aid of an open-
ended schedule followed experimentation with a more structured
tool, the multiple choice questionnaire. The open-ended or semi-
structured schedule was eventually decided upon for several reasons: It is usable both as an interview schedule in the questioning
of respondents and as a schedule for ordering available data such
as are found in agency case records, psychiatric protocols, diaries,
etc. It permits the bringing together of information from multiple
sources. It also makes possible the collection of pertinent data
from heterogeneous samples of families. The latter point is important when the specific nature of the families to be studied is
not yet known. When structured instruments are constructed, on
the other hand, it is presupposed that prior research has determined
the precise universe of content to be collected. That means, in
effect, that different structured instruments might be needed if the
samples vary in structure or function, or a single comprehensive
instrument would be required, one that anticipates all response
possibilities--a product that is bound to be lengthy. There is additional advantage to the open-ended schedule. It can be used in
an informal interviewer-respondent exchange which maximizes the
chances of motivating the respondent to volunteer information.

Contraposed to the advantages of the open-ended schedule
are some disadvantages, as every experienced researcher knows.
The data collection process is harder to standardize. Coding is
more difficult. Some of the controls that can be applied in the
gathering of pre-structured data are missing. Nevertheless, the
problems inherent in constructing one bulky, comprhensive questionnaire or smaller, separate forms for each new study are greater
than the difficulties presented by the semi-structured schedule.
Perhaps the major prerequisite for its successful use is the a-
vailability of skilled and well-trained interviewers. Because the
items in the schedule are more general than questionnaire items,
they require translating into a more specific format. For instance,

"social outlets of family members" under the area heading Social
Activities and sub-heading Informal Associations needs to supply
the answers to such questions as the following: What do family
members do for sociability? How do they enjoy themselves?
What informal groups do they belong to? How long do the associations last? It follows that interviewers using the open-ended schedule have to understand very clearly the meaning of abstract formulations about family functioning, so that they may be able to trans-
late them into the meaningful and relevant items called for in each
situation.

     If the open-ended schedule is used it is necessary to have
the interview conducted in a relaxed and informal atmosphere where
the respondent can answer freely. The interviewer can encourage
freedom of expression by letting the respondent move from subject
to subject in a manner he considers most meaningful. Notes may
be taken inconspicuously or the interview may be taped (with permission of the respondent) in order to minimize interference with
the flow of information. Thorough knowledge of the schedule will
enable the interviewer to request--unobtrusively--items of information not yet covered without breaking the continuity of the exchange.
It is also possible to divide interviews into several sessions, thereby reducing respondent fatigue. It has been our experience that
the skillfully conducted interview generally represents a pleasant
experience for the interviewee; there have been very few break-
offs once the respondent has been engaged in discussion.

     We have found that it is necessary for interviewers using
the schedule on Family Functioning to have had prior experience
in handling family data in a conceptual manner. Furthermore,
trial interviews should be carried out, in which the interviewer
can demonstrate his or her ability to motivate the respondent and
to guide him in supplying the relevant material. If available information is used, the data collector needs to supply evidence of
his ability to select appropriate content from that which is given.
The kind of unstructured interviewing this schedule demands leaves
more room for the injection of interviewer bias than does structured

interviewing, and the interviewer needs a fair measure of sophisti-
cation to guard against this.

The narrative account of a family's social functioning, organized by areas and sub-areas, will be referred to as the Profile
of Family Functioning.   The outline used for writing the Profile,
tested through the study of hundreds of families, has been found
to be a reasonably comprehensive instrument able to gather information about the average family whether young or old, rich or
poor, stable or disorganized.   At the same time, we must concede
that this outline is general and may need to be modified for the
study of specific populations or problems.   We have on various
occasions set up modified forms covering one area or another, as
the need arises.   For example, it was found that a substitute schedule for the sub-area Marital Relationship is helpful in research with
out-of-wedlock mothers.   Likewise, in the study of families with
children in institutions, a special schedule for Individual Behavior
and Adjustment - Children Placed was required.   That schedule
included special items dealing with the child's experience in the
institution and with various psychological dimensions of child
development which constituted an important aspect of that particular study.

The interviewer or collector of data from available information will rarely find information on every single item listed in the
schedule.   Where seemingly essential items are not known, it
should be noted in the narrative according to instructions given
below.   The coder of the Profile of Family Functioning will have
to decide whether or not there is sufficient information to code a
particular category.   On the other hand, the Profile writer may
wish to collect relevant information beyond that requested in the
outline.   There is always room for such, especially since the
writer makes no claim for completeness.   A substantial extension
of data collection which is clearly over and above the requirements
of the schedule had best be done with the aid of a revised form,
the content of which is dictated by the needs of the study.

The first two areas in the outline contain a sub-section

called "History." Under A. Family Relationships and Family
Unity, the collection of historic information applies only to the
Marital Relationship, while under B. Individual Behavior and Adjustment, history refers to the functioning of each family member
except a newborn. The historic data supply background knowledge
for rating present functioning, but they are not rated by themselves.
There is no way to determine exactly how extensive the information
on the background of marriage and individual behavior needs to be
in order to make rating of present functioning most meaningful.
Some information, it would seem, it indispensable in order to code
present behavior within a broader context of cultural norms and
expectations, but complete data on every item under family history
should be regarded as optional.

By far the most important set of instructions for profiling
family functioning pertains to the nature of reporting. The Profile
calls essentially for descriptive information on all aspects covered
by the categories and sub-categories. Evaluative statements or
diagnostic terminology is to be avoided except as it can be documented by a description of the actual behavior or situation or by
the results of objective assessments in the form of tests, examinations, school grades, and the like. Members of the helping professions, such as social work, clinical psychology, and psychiatry,
who are prone to assemble diagnostic material that is problem-
focused, may need to be reminded that when writing the Profile
of Family Functioning comparable emphasis must be given to the
strengths as well as the weaknesses in family life.

A question frequently asked is whether, in instances where
the collection of family functioning data is tied to a service project,
research information should be collected by the person rendering
the services. This writer observed that most researchers almost
instinctively tend to respond to this suggestion in a negative manner. The danger of lack of objectivity on the part of a worker
who is professionally involved with or committed to a respondent
is usually cited. There is little doubt that the dangers of mixing
and possibly confusing the roles of researcher and practitioner are

real. Therefore, we would tend to adhere to the general rule of thumb calling for role separation and the employment of interviewers to work independently from the service practitioner.

There is, nonetheless, another consideration which must enter a decision on this matter. If the interviewing is to be effective it is highly desirable that a positive relationship exist between interviewer and respondent. The entry of a research interviewer into a situation where a treatment worker has already been gathering comparable information may constitute a demand which the respondent resents or rejects. His response may range all the way from outright refusal to a more subtle withholding of full cooperation. The latter could take the form of not giving all the information the interviewer is seeking or of giving biased information, and this need not be deliberate but may take a subconscious form.

When making a decision on who will gather the research data, the risk of getting biased data must be weighed against the other, and sometimes greater, risk of obtaining superficial or incomplete data, which may be biased as well. A solution to this dilemma may take several forms. The research project and the service worker may make special efforts from the beginning of treatment to prepare the respondent, who is also a client, for the entry of the research interviewer, and special incentives in the form of monetary rewards or the sharing of research information may be provided to maximize the chances for client collaboration. An alternative to this arrangement, to be employed when it is impossible to separate research interviewers for all cases, is to set up special controls to reduce bias in the data collection of practitioners. These may include a tighter structuring of the research schedule, additional training for practitioners in research interviewing, and the application of quality control techniques by comparing--through duplicate interviewing--the data collected by practitioners with those gathered by a research interviewer on every Nth case in the study.

IV.   4.   Outline for Preparing a Profile of Family Functioning

General Instructions:

The information to be gathered under the outline headings should be written on sheets of paper which are blank except for a listing of the capitalized headings (areas of family functioning preceded by a capital letter) and underlined headings (sub-areas preceded by numerals, also history and present functioning).   Three pages each should be reserved for areas A (Family Relationships and Family Unity) and B (Individual Behavior and Adjustment), while one page will suffice for each of the remaining areas or main categories.

One Profile constitutes a cross-sectional picture of family functioning, i. e. , a documentation of social functioning during a limited time span.   The first Profile also includes historical information on the marriage and on the individual behavior of family members, which need not be repeated in the second and--if applicable--subsequent Profiles.   However, the Profiles following the first should report under each heading developments which have occurred since the writing of the previous Profile.   If there have been no changes whatsoever since the previous write-up, this also should be noted.

Seek to cover every item of information, particularly in relation to the family's present functioning.   Whenever it is found that an item is not applicable--such as Relationship Among Children when there is but one child--note this by using the initials N. A. (not applicable).   Whenever you are unable to provide information because the interviewer failed to obtain it or because it was not found in the available data, use the initials N. K. , indicating that the information is not known.

Data collection under area H. Relationship to Social Worker, or to another professional practitioner carrying out social intervention, is only appropriate if a special intervention program was taking place at the time of the study or if the family in question

was being studied by the agency rendering treatment services.
Where this is not the case but families happen to be receiving
psychotherapy or another form of helping service, that fact can
be recorded under B.   Individual Behavior and Adjustment and L
Use of Community Resources.

    The need for descriptive, nonevaluative reporting in Profile
writing cannot be stressed too heavily.   Where evaluative statements are used, they must be backed up by examples of the behavior or functioning leading to the use of these concepts.   Diagnostic terminology should be employed only when supported by test
scores, results of examinations, or expert judgment.   The outline
itself follows below.

Outline for Profiling Family Functioning

A. FAMILY RELATIONSHIPS AND FAMILY UNITY

    1. Marital Relationship

        a. History

        Circumstances leading to marriage: how did you meet?
            when? where? was there a formal engagement? what
            made you decide to get married? how did both sets
            of parents feel about the marriage? when were you
            married? where? who performed the ceremony?

        Post marital adjustment - first years: where did you
            live?   how far from husband's or wife's parents?
            how often did you exchange visits?   how did you get
            along with parents and in-laws?   job situation; fi-
            nancial resources; emotional and social adjustment;
            sexual adjustment and relative importance of sex in
            married life; use of birth control; how many children
            do you desire?   how would you prefer (have preferred)
            to space them?

        Early image of marriage: agreement or discrepancy be-
            tween image before marriage and actual experience;
            degree of realism of pre-marital image; knowledge
            of sex before marriage; source of such knowledge;
            pre-marital sex experience.

        Arrival of first child: planned vs. unplanned pregnancy;
            physical and emotional health of mother during preg-
            nancy; husband's and wife's attitudes toward child

during pregnancy and after his (her) arrival.

b. Present Functioning

Degree of love and compatibility: how well do the partners get along generally? agreement or disagreement
in tastes, interests, views, temperaments.

Closeness of emotional ties vs. estrangement and conflict:
what kind of emotional relationship? what does wife
expect and what does she get regarding tenderness,
demonstrated affection, considerateness of feelings,
moods, irritations, off-days, temper? same for husband - what does he expect of wife? what does he
get?

Interdependence and independence between partners; degree
of sharing; talking out feelings; agreements and disagreements, both regarding marriage and outside affairs.

Sources of satisfaction and dissatisfaction: inside and outside marriage, as regards friends, relatives, job,
social and cultural pursuits; family goals: what do
spouses want on a long term basis?

Agreements and disagreements: their sources; who makes
decisions? about what? what are the results? is
there a division of labor? what is its nature and how
satisfactory is it? any other differences, disagreements, or problems? how are they handled?

Sexual adjustment: frequency of sex relations; how important and how satisfying to each?

Responsibility for financial support: who bears it? how
well is it met?

Extra-marital relationships: how long in progress? how
casual or intensive? is marriage partner aware of it
and how has he or she reacted?

Mutual role expectations: what does the wife see as her
husband's and her own duties and responsibilities?
how does the husband see this? do their views agree
or differ? what are the effects?

Part played by separated partners: if couple is separated,
give detailed description of present relationship; extent to which legal obligations are met.

2. Relationship Between Parents and Children

Degree of affection between children and parents.

Display vs. concealment of emotions: how are they displayed - holding and cuddling, playing, etc. ? amount of care and helping done by the husband, if any; how satisfying is arrangement for care and discipline to each partner?

Degree of respect of children for parents.

Parents' respect for children's rights; how much understanding does each parent have of infantile behavior, i. e., the demands and needs of young children, especially when it interferes with parents' comfort and freedom?

Indifference or rejection.

Favoritism shown by parents.

Companionship and shared activities: what kind of activities does each parent share with the children?

3. Relationship Among Children

Degree of closeness, loyalty, affection among children.

Pride in sibling's achievements.

Playing patterns, sharing of possessions.

Cooperation vs. resentment.

Areas of agreement and conflict: fighting, teasing, bullying.

4. Family Solidarity

Sense of family identity: cohesiveness vs. individual solitude and isolation of family members; do the members of the family generally "go it together" or is there a pattern of going separate ways?

Reciprocal values, goals, and expectations: values shared vs. values that divide the family.

Family traditions and ritual, shared customs: what, if any, are family traditions? this might include what may have been adopted from their own parents and is still shared with them.

Degree of affection and emotional warmth vs. conflict and indifference among family members.

Pride in family, pulling together in times of stress.

Shared activities: meals, recreation, travel; planning for common goals.

Nature of decision-making process: is it individual or group?

The use of cultural media such as movies, T. V. , radio, books, magazines, etc. , as part of family life.

5. Relationship with Other Household Members

Nature of relationships with household members (specify who they are) who are not part of the nuclear family.

Degree to which other household members share in or are excluded from family life.

Benefits and problems inherent in a combined living arrangement: who benefits and who is harmed? in what manner? effect of arrangement on family's economic situation, sense of identity.

B. INDIVIDUAL BEHAVIOR AND ADJUSTMENT

Under separate headings cover the behavior and adjustment of 1. Father, 2. Mother, 3. Oldest child at home, 4. Second oldest child, 5. Third oldest child, etc. For each individual list birthdates after first name and date(s) of marriage where applicable. Divide the narrative on each family member into two parts: 1. history, and 2. present functioning.

1. History

Structure of family of orientation; nativity of parents; religion of parents; amount of education of parents; size of family; one or both parents in the home; number of siblings; ordinal position of respondent; out-of-wedlock children.

Social and emotional atmosphere of parental home; affection and solidarity vs. conflict; marital relationship of parents; relationship to parents; sibling relationships; health of parents; separations or other crises in family; basic values of the home (religious, ethical, levels of aspiration).

Socio-economic status of parental home: occupation and income; regularity of income; work patterns; type of residence (rural-urban); characteristics of neighborhood; pattern of social activities.

Education, training, and job experience of husband and
wife prior to marriage; type of schools attended;
reasons for leaving school; occupational training;
jobs held before marriage; talents and hobbies.

Social adjustment before present marriage; type of adjustment at home and after leaving home (if applicable);
social, emotional, and health problems; delinquency
and other deviant behavior; social activities and leisure;
patterns of dating; social status of siblings.

2. Present Functioning

a. Factors to be considered for PARENTS (family
of procreation)

General characteristics: appearance, mannerisms, personality traits, ideas, values, attitudes, interests,
education, and intelligence levels. Give brief physical
description of each parent.

Social behavior: adaptive behavior, social skills, relationships with people and institutions; social conformity
vs. deviance; handicapping traits and attitudes; law
violations; drinking, drug addiction, deviant sexual behavior; other forms of deviant behavior.

Mental-physical state: personality structure, mental
health, emotional disorder, internal conflict, mental
retardation, chronic and/or serious disease.

Role performance: as spouse, breadwinner, homemaker,
neighbor, member of the community, participant in
trade and professional associations, member of clubs,
lodges, special programs, etc. ; nature and degree of
role involvement; acceptance vs. rejection by role
partners; personal competence for role playing; degree
of satisfaction derived. Draw on agency records,
psychiatric evaluations, police and probation records
as well as your own observations.

b. Factors to be considered for CHILDREN:

General characteristics: same as for parents.

Social behavior: same as for parents.

Mental-physical state: same as for parents.

Role performance: as child in home setting, sibling, pupil,
member of peer groups, play groups, etc. ; nature and
degree of role involvement; acceptance vs. rejection

by role partners; personal competence for role playing; degree of satisfaction derived. Draw on school
and camp reports, psychiatric and psychological sum-
maries, test results, police and probation records, as
well as your own observations.

C. CARE AND TRAINING OF CHILDREN

1. Physical Care

Physical appearance.

Supply and condition of clothing.

Nutrition.

Attention given to cleanliness, diet, and health needs.

In the case of infants, give the schedule of the mother's
care.

2. Training Methods and Emotional Care

Affection, indifference, rejection, rigidity, overpermissive-
ness.

Kind of punishment used (or contemplated in the case of
an infant): appropriateness of discipline to behavior;
discipline by whom, for what? consistency of discipline,
family rules; agreement between parents over exercise
of discipline; approval of good conduct (whether given).

Encouragement of independence vs. fostering of independence.

Differential treatment of siblings.

Behavior standards set by parents.

D. SOCIAL ACTIVITIES

1. Informal Associations

Relationships with parents, in-laws, friends and neighbors:
their nature and frequency.

Social outlets of family members.

Anti-social acts; their nature and motivation.

Identification with larger groups, i.e., neighborhood, community.

Socialization experience for children beyond the nuclear family.

Ways in which free time is spent informally.

2. Formal Associations

Membership of family members in organized groups (social, economic, political, and recreational).

Attitude toward organized groups and activities (include unions, lodges, religious groups, etc.).

Type of activity in groups: nominal memberships vs. leadership or committee memberships.

Degree of satisfaction derived from formal associations.

E.   ECONOMIC PRACTICES

1.   Source(s) and Amount of Family Income

Employment, public assistance, insurance, support from relatives.

Adequacy of income relative to family's needs.

Satisfaction with income.

Necessities provided?

2.   Job Situation (applies to family members who contribute substantially to support of family)

Nature of work, employment practices.

Behavior on job, attitude toward employment.

Relations with boss and co-workers.

Satisfaction or dissatisfaction with job.

Suitability of job for person's capabilities.

Frequency of job changes.

Reaction of wife and children to job situation.

3.   Use of Money

Ability to manage money: who manages the money? who

decides on expenditures? agreement vs. disagreement over money management.

Budgeting: haphazard or systematic? use of banks, methods of saving, insurances.

Priorities for spending money: realistic regard to basic necessities?

Amount and nature of debts, reason for debts.

F. HOME AND HOUSEHOLD PRACTICES

1. Physical Facilities

Type of home, age, ownership (public, private), number of rooms, arrangement of rooms, privacy, crowding.

Physical condition of home.

Characteristics of neighborhood: types of buildings and their age; conditions of buildings and yards; nature of street scene: traffic, people on the streets, cleanliness, etc.

Adequacy of basic household equipment: furnishings for sleeping, bathing, refrigeration, cooking, sanitation.

Attitude toward home: attention to making it attractive vs. neglect.

2. Housekeeping Standards

Management of household chores: how assigned, executed?

Ways of serving meals and adequacy of diet; timing and regularity of meals.

Buying patterns: food, clothing, recreation, car, furniture, etc.

Neatness of home: pride vs. indifference regarding management of the household.

G. HEALTH CONDITIONS AND PRACTICES

1. Health Conditions (include a paragraph on each family member)

Health of family members: adequate, normal functioning?

problems, diseases, handicaps, debilitating conditions, mental illness?

2. Health Practices

Medical care obtained or avoided?

Use of preventive resources: well-baby clinic, T. B., X-Ray.

Care exercised in following medical instructions?

Disease prevention practices; physical hygiene practices.

Dental care: regularity, hygiene.

H. RELATIONSHIP TO SOCIAL WORKER (See General Instructions)

1. Attitude toward Worker

Opinions expressed by client family; attitudes reflected in their behavior; is family co-operative, indifferent, hostile, suspicious, etc. ? which family members reveal what kinds of attitudes toward professional intervention?

2. Use of Worker

Manner in which client uses worker: for advice, guidance, concrete help, dealing with problems, venting feelings, manipulation, etc. what does client expect from worker?

I. USE OF COMMUNITY RESOURCES

1. School (include primary, secondary, and adult education)

Value parents place on education, their attitudes toward the school.

Interest they take in children's school activities, contact with school personnel.

Children's attitudes toward school, achievement, attendance, behavior.

2. Church (check "not appropriate" if no contact or nominal tie only)

Membership and attendance; denomination.

Type of participation: services, Sunday School, church clubs, etc.

Satisfaction derived from attendance.

Agreement of parents on children's participation.

Influence of church membership on family solidarity.

3.   Health Resources (include only physical health)

Type of services used: public; private; clinics; out-patient departments; etc.

Knowledge about and attitude toward resources: cooperative; apathetic; suspicious; hostile; resentful; etc.

Use of agencies: appointments kept or missed; medical advice used or disregarded.

4.   Social Agencies (include penal and correctional services such as Probation and Parole, Housing Authorities, employment agencies, Public Welfare, family planning services, social adjustment services - general and sectarian, mental health and hygiene clinics, etc.)

Knowledge about and attitude toward agencies; well or poorly informed; favorable attitudes; hostile; resentful; apathetic; defensive; etc.

Use of agencies: source of referral; family seeks help; is cooperative; uses agency appropriately; overly demanding; refuses to accept agency services; etc.

5.   Recreational Agencies (include clubs, community and neighborhood centers, organized playgrounds, public and private recreation programs and services, recreation camps, etc.)

Knowledge and use made of recreational agencies by children; frequency and regularity of use.

Parents' use of and attitude toward recreational facilities for children and adults.

Additional Instructions for Profile Writing

(1)   The first step to be taken when writing a Profile of Family Functioning is to thoroughly review all areas or main categories and sub-categories.   This will enable the writer, whether interviewer or arranger of available data, to organize the informa-

tion in a manner that fits the Profile structure. An interviewer who has already conducted the interview and has thus become acquainted with the schedule will have to rearrange his handwritten notes or the tape recorded transcript. If the information is being taken from available data, some time will be needed to reorganize them to fit the Profile format.

(2) The first Profile which covers information gathered at the start of the study should be written with a clear terminal date in mind. Information beyond that date belongs to the second Profile, or to subsequent ones. Conversely, interview material secured in second, third, or later interviews may be found to belong under the beginning situation covered in the first Profile, even though it was not picked up in the initial interview. Room should, therefore, be left in the first Profile for appropriate additions.

(3) Cross-referencing of information helps avoid repetition. Areas and sub-areas are organized to minimize duplication but some overlapping is unavoidable. For instance, the physical disability of the father, the main wage earner, deserves mention under Individual Behavior and Adjustment, Health Conditions and Practices, and Economic Practices. Other areas such as Family Relationships and Unity and Social Activities may be affected. A detailed description of the condition, however, need not be given under more than one heading and can be cross-referenced under the others.

(4) The first Profile is the most truly cross-sectional in nature, for it covers the beginning situation which can be defined as the social functioning of a family during a given time span--let us say a three or four-week period--preceding the first interview. For certain kinds of officially recorded behavior, such as institutionalizations, incarcerations, court convictions, etc., it seems appropriate to include in the first Profile information covering the past year. Subsequent Profiles are cross-sectional, with a latitude covering the time span from the previous Profile. Ideally, the time span should not exceed six months since the accumulation of data for a longer period of time makes rating more difficult. Within the limited time span the Profile is, therefore, a "moving

picture" rather than a "snapshot." Thus, if at the time of interviewing a child is behaving normally but has been in trouble frequently during previous months, the "snapshot" type of reporting would give a skewed picture whereas a description of the longer trend of behavior would give a truer picture of his functioning.

IV. 5. Rating Family Functioning

   A well written Profile is the prerequisite for an effective
evaluation of a family's social functioning. The next step in the
evaluative process is the rating of the case narrative, but rating
is possible only after the criteria by which the rating or coding is
to be done are spelled out.

   Chart I had listed four criteria on dimensions that are the
composite measure for coding family functioning. The criteria
take two forms: (1) General criteria, formulated at a high level
of abstraction and applicable to all areas of family functioning;
(2) Specific criteria, expressed at a somewhat lower level of abstraction and relevant to areas and sub-areas of family functioning.
The four dimensions of functioning, as stated earlier, are not
equally represented in each category for the simple reason that
criteria of health and welfare and conformity-deviance are not of
equal significance in every type of behavior, role playing, or task
performance. The issue of conformity-deviance, for example, is
likely to figure prominently in a child's student role but is of very
minor importance in the planning and serving of meals. Regarding
the latter, the question of nutritional balance (health dimension) is,
of course, the major issue guiding the ratings on social functioning.

   In line with the overall purposes of evaluation, general as
well as specific criteria for coding social functioning need to be
laid out on an evaluative continuum, ranging from the most positive
to the most negative or the most favorable to the most unfavorable,
depending on whichever concepts are appropriate to the study. The
researchers in the St. Paul Family Centered Project decided to
select the designation adequate/inadequate to denote the extremes
of the continuum for measurement.

   Adequate functioning denotes behavior and situations most
conducive to the welfare of the family and its members, while
inadequate functioning signifies the opposite. Inadequate functioning
is seen as so damaging to the family and/or society as to entitle
the community to intervene. Adequate functioning, by contrast, is

seen to be in line with community expectations. Adequate and inadequate functioning represent the extreme positions on a seven-
point continuum whose midpoint or anchor position is marginal
functioning, defined as behavior and situations that are potentially
problematic but not sufficiently harmful to justify community intervention on legal grounds. The in-between positions--near adequate,
above marginal, below marginal, and near inadequate--represent
levels of functioning slightly higher or lower than the others which
are spelled out in the criteria for rating functioning. The general
criteria for rating family functioning are given on the next page
and are followed by a listing of specific criteria by area and sub-
area.

Criteria for Rating Family Functioning[15]

I. General Criteria.

Inadequate	Marginal	Adequate
Functioning Harmful to the Point Where Community Has a Right to Intervene	Functioning Not Sufficiently Harmful to Justify Intervention	Functioning is in Line with Community Expectations
Laws and/or mores are clearly violated. Behavior of family members is a threat to the community.	Major laws are not being violated, although behavior of family members is at variance with status group expectations.	Laws are obeyed and mores observed. Behavior is in line with status group expectations.
Family life is characterized by extreme conflict, neglect, severe deprivation, unhappiness or very poor relationships resulting in physical and/or emotional suffering of family members; disruption of family life is imminent; children are in clear and present danger because of above conditions or other behavior inimical to their welfare.	Family life is generally marked by conflict, apathy, or unstable relationships which can be seen as a potential threat to the family's and/or the community's welfare. Family is poorly equipped to deal with problems; family members are frequently dissatisfied with their condition and do not possess the knowledge or ability to improve it. Although children are not being properly socialized and their environment is not fully conducive to healthy physical or emotional development, they are not in imminent danger.	Family members are generally satisfied with their lot, and their needs are being met. Efforts aimed at improvement are made where appropriate. Family life is stable; members have a sense of belonging and sharing mutually compatible goals and expectations. Problems are faced and dealt with appropriately. Children are being raised in an atmosphere conducive to healthy growth and development. Socialization process stresses positive mental health, preparation for present and future roles and the acquisition of social skills.

II. Specific Criteria.

A. FAMILY RELATIONSHIPS AND FAMILY UNITY

1. Marital Relationship

Marital Relationship should be checked where either or both of the
following are applicable: 1) One partner has legal responsibility toward the
other, has some contact with the family or exerts some influence on it;

2) There is a continuing extra-marital relationship of significance in family functioning.

When rating a family headed by an O. W. (out-of-wedlock) mother, code the relationship between the unmarried mother and the father of her child(ren).   However, if there is a sustained, ongoing relationship between her and any other "significant male" (other than members of her family) rate the quality of that relationship.   (A "significant" other is one with whom there is a continuing, emotional relationship and who asserts some influence on the family system.)

Check Not Applicable wherever above elements are not present.

Inadequate	Marginal	Adequate
Partner, whether or not separated, does not support them when so ordered or is extremely disturbing influence on family.	Partner, whether or not separated, does not support adequately or is a disturbing influence in family.	Couple lives together, derives satisfaction from their relationship.
Extra-marital relations are endangering children's welfare, or have come to attention of law.	Extra-marital relations exist but do not openly affect welfare of children, or pose immediate threat to family solidarity.	There is a positive emotional tie between partners who can both express need for the other's help and respond appropriately when the other requires help. Considerable pleasure is derived from shared experiences.
Emotional tie so deficient that children are endangered.	Weak emotional tie between partners, lack of concern for each other.	There is a consistent effort to limit the scope and duration of marital conflict and to keep communication open for resolution of conflicts which arise.
Severe, persistent marital conflict necessitates intervention by authorities or threatens a complete disruption of family life.	There are some points of agreement between partners, but disagreement and conflict tend to predominate.	

2. Relationship Between Parents and Children

Inadequate	Marginal	Adequate
No affection is shown between parents and children. There is great indifference or marked rejection of children. No respect is shown for one another. No approval, recognition, or encouragement is shown to children. If any concern is shown at all by parents, it takes the form of rank discrimination in favor of a few against the rest. Parent-child conflict is extremely severe. (Above so serious as to constitute neglect or abuse as legally defined, warranting community intervention.)	Affection between parents and children is intermittent, or weak, or obscured by conflict. Parents' anger is unpredictable and unrelated to specific conduct of children. Family members are played off against each other. There is marked favoritism with no attempt to compensate disadvantaged children. There is little mutual respect or concern for each other. Parents and children are frequently in conflict. Parents of very young children are indifferent in handling or assuming responsibility for them. (Danger to children is potential not actual.)	Affection is shown between parents and children. Parents try always to be consistent in treatment of children. Children have sense of belonging, emotional security. Children and parents show respect for each other, mutual concern. Parent-child conflict is minimal or restricted by consistent attention, free communication, and desire for harmony. Parents of very young children derive satisfaction from caring for them, and assume major role in their care.

3. Sibling Relationships

Pertains only to relationships among natural or adopted siblings.

Inadequate	Marginal	Adequate
There is conflict between children resulting in physical violence or cruelty which warrants intervention.	Emotional ties among children are weak. Rarely play together. Fighting occurs, often teasing, bullying, other types of emotional or physical cruelty. Children rarely share playthings, show little loyalty to one another or pride in other's achievements.	There are positive emotional ties and mutual identification among children. Depending on age, often play together, share their playthings. Are loyal to each other, enjoy other's company, take pride in achievements of their siblings. Fighting and bickering are normal for age.

4. Family Solidarity

In families headed by O. W. mothers the concept covers the relationship between the mother and her natural child(ren). In addition, her relationship to her parents (natural, step, or surrogate) is covered providing they live in the same household. If the unmarried mother lives with other family members, code under Relationship With Other Household Members. Relationships with extended family not living in same household are rated under Informal Associations.

Inadequate	Marginal	Adequate
There is marked lack of affection and emotional ties among family members. Conflict among members is persistent or severe.	Little emotional warmth is evidenced among family members. Family members are often in conflict.	Warmth and affection are shown among family members, giving them a sense of belonging and emotional security. Conflict within family is dealt with quickly and appropriately.
There is marked lack of cohesiveness and mutual concern; satisfactions in family living are not evident. There is no pride in family or sense of family identity. Members plan on basis of personal gratification rather than for family as whole. There is serious danger of family disruption. (Above is so serious that laws relating to neglect or cruelty are violated or family welfare is so threatened that intervention is justified.) Family solidarity assumes antisocial forms.	There is little cohesiveness; for example, members rarely do things together; there is little planning toward common family goals; little feeling of collective responsibility; little pulling together in crisis. There are few satisfactions in family living. (Above potential but not yet actual danger to welfare of children.)	There is definitive evidence of cohesiveness; for example, members often do things together; eat together; family plans and works toward some common goals; there is definite feeling of collective responsibility; members pull together in times of stress. Members find considerable satisfaction in family living. Cohesiveness is not at odds with the welfare of the community.

5. Relationships with Other Household Members

Inadequate	Marginal	Adequate
Relationships are marked by hostilities, sometimes resulting in physical and verbal battles. The purloining of each other's personal property, disregard of privacy, or frequent fighting has resulted in, or warrants, outside intervention. Household members studiously ignore one another or treat each other with contempt. Various cruelties result in serious emotional or physical injuries to one or more household members.	Household members resent one another's presence, and do not respect other adults' rights to privacy. Disputes are frequent, shown either by verbal bickering, petty jealousy, or ignoring of one another. Some adults refuse to take responsibilities for household, such as contributing their share to general expenses or helping with household chores, to the resentment of others.	Adults in household group treat each other with consideration and mutual concern. Conflicts and misunderstandings are usually recognized and settled quickly and appropriately.
Conflict among children is severe, persistent, and violent. Adults show marked preference of one child over another, resulting in serious deprivation and problems warranting community intervention. Parents strongly resent presence of children in home and openly show their hostilities.	Children rarely play together or share playthings. Fighting among children is frequent but does not result in physical harm to one another.

Adults show little concern or affection for children, barely tolerate their presence in household. | Children in household group like to play together, don't mind sharing toys, sports equipment, etc. Disputes and bickering among children are not out of line for their age group.

Adults in household group do not show favoritism or marked preference for some child(ren) over others. Adults do not mind the presence of children in household. |

B. INDIVIDUAL BEHAVIOR AND ADJUSTMENT

1. Individual Behavior and Adjustment of Parents

Check separately for mother and father. Check "Not Applicable" (N. A.) if absent parent has no tie to family (as indicated under marital relationship). If there is more than one mother or father figure with ties to family, check the one who has the strongest tie. Check "inadequate" if consequences of law violations (incarceration, probation, etc.) are still operative; however, prolonged probation should be weighed with other factors.

For Unmarried Mothers:

Father: Should be rated only if there had been a rating in the sub-
         category Marital Relationships. "Father" again pertains to
         either the biological father of the OW child, or a "significant"
         other as defined in Marital Relationships.

Mother: The presence of an out-of-wedlock child is not in itself a basis
         for a lower rating on the mother. In this sub-category we are
         rating the mother's behavior and her functioning in various roles,
         such as parent, homemaker, member of the community, etc.,
         all of which contribute to the numerical rating of the other's
         Individual Behavior and Adjustment.

Inadequate	Marginal	Adequate
Social Behavior	Social Behavior	Social Behavior
Is incarcerated or on probation for law violation. Seriously deviant sexual behavior (promiscuity, etc.) or serious offenses against family (assault, incest, etc.) endanger welfare of children. Excessive drinking, consumption of drugs severely affects family welfare (reducing budget below minimal level, causing severe conflict, etc.) and warrants intervention for sake of children.	Minor law violations do not result in incarceration or probation; there are instances of deviant sexual conduct, offenses against family, or excessive drinking and taking of drugs but they do not seriously affect family welfare. Deficiency in social skills handicaps comfortable relationships to people and institutions.	Law violations are limited to such slight infractions as minor traffic violations. Has good supplement of social skills, relates comfortably to most people and institutions.
Mental-Physical	Mental-Physical	Mental-Physical
Serious mental illness requires intervention or results in institutionalization.	Mental or emotional disorder is present but individual functions on minimal level, not actually dangerous to family; little personal satisfaction is experienced in life. Individual is forced to function below the level of his potential.	Mental health good, has positive self image. Psycho-social functioning is at the level of individual's potential. Is satisfied with his situation and social roles.
Mental defectiveness requires institutionalization or so limits capacity as to disrupt family life; special help or training is needed but not provided.		Performs up to mental capacity and is able to function satisfactorily in most areas.
Parent has disease which endangers	Chronic or major physical disease or handicap is somewhat disabling but permits	No diseases or handicaps of serious nature;

public health and en-
titles health authorities
to intervene; has not
sought or carried
through on treatment;
chronic or major physi-
cal disease or handicap
is so disabling that per-
son is unable to provide
minimum care for chil-
dren who are his major
responsibility.

minimal functioning,
especially in regard
to care of children.

receiving appropriate
treatment, where neces-
sary; functioning ham-
pered only slightly if
at all.

Role Performance:*

Role Performance:*

Role Performance:*

As Spouse: If deserted
or separated, does not
support when so or-
dered. Extra-marital
liaisons endanger fam-
ily. Severe conflict
with spouse is damag-
ing to children.

As Spouse: There is
frequent conflict or
disagreement with spouse
in many areas of living;
emotional tie is weak.

As Spouse: Conflict
with spouse is mini-
mal, dealt with ap-
propriately; there is
positive emotional tie;
disagreements are well
handled or well tolera-
ted.

As Parent: There is
violation of laws re-
lating to neglect of
children, assault, in-
cest, etc., making in-
tervention necessary.

As Parent: There is
little concern for or
interest in children.
Displays little affec-
tion for them; mini-
mal physical and emo-
tional care are pro-
vided. Some favorit-
ism is shown.

As Parent: There is
positive relationship
with children; shows
them affection, spends
time with them, pro-
vides appropriate physi-
cal and emotional care.

As Breadwinner: If ab-
sent, does not support
when so ordered. If at
home, and physically
and mentally able to
work, is unwilling to
support family.

As Breadwinner: Pro-
vides minimal or un-
certain income, but
little or no PA re-
quired (unless so
disabled as to require
outside support).

As Breadwinner: Pro-
vides income for family
which meets their needs
satisfactorily. Works
regularly at job, has
positive feeling for it.

As Homemaker: House-
keeping and care of
children is so inadequate
that it constitutes neglect
and warrants intervention.

As Homemaker: House-
keeping and care of
children is generally
poor, and person is
disinterested in home-
maker role.

As Homemaker: House-
keeping and care of
children is good, and
person derives satis-
faction from homemaker
role.

As Member of Com-
munity: There are
law violations other
than offenses against
family. Extremely
hostile attitude toward
community--children
are encouraged to com-
mit anti-social acts.

As Member of Com-
munity: Has little
or no social con-
tacts with neighbors,
relatives, etc.; be-
longs to no social
groups, is dissatis-
fied with social
status. Makes poor

As Member of Com-
munity: Has meaning-
ful ties with friends,
relatives, etc. Belongs
to some social groups
which provide satisfac-
tions, is comfortable
with standing in com-
munity. Has positive

use of resources, is ignorant of, or apathetic toward resources when need exists to use them.	attitude toward community, makes good use of facilities when necessary. Strivings toward upward mobility are kept within realistic bounds.

---

*Due allowance should be made for variations in parental roles made nececessary by the particular family structure. Thus the mother's role as supplementary or chief wage earner needs to be considered where children do not have to be looked after during the day. The father's role as homemaker may have to be taken into account where he is unable to earn a living, etc.

2. Individual Behavior and Adjustment of Children

For purposes of scoring, children 10 and over are considered together, as are children from 1-9. The total score for each group is determined by finding the weighted average of separate scores. Do not consider children who are permanently out of the home. Rate only the natural or adoptive children of the nuclear family or unmarried mother. (In studies that focus on the functioning of the children, each child should be rated separately for purposes of furnishing score outputs in which each sibling can be treated as a variable.)

Inadequate	Marginal	Adequate
Acting Out Behavior:	Acting Out Behavior:	Acting Out Behavior:
Acting out, disruptive, anti-social behavior is of serious concern and indicative of a child in real danger, warranting intervention. Incarcerated or on probation.	Acting out, disruptive, or anti-social behavior is not a long or continuous pattern.	Acting out behavior is normal for age; pranks, mischievousness, etc. , not of serious nature.
Mental-Physical State:	Mental-Physical State:	Mental-Physical State:
Mental illness requires intervention or results in hospitalization. Excessive withdrawal, heavy drinking, drug addiction, or other behavior suggests emotional disturbance or serious problems in relating to others.	Emotional disorder is evident, but receiving treatment or not serious enough to justify intervention; little personal satisfaction is experienced in life. Performance is below mental and/or physical capacity. Mental	Emotional health appears good, has positive self-image, enjoys appropriate activites, relates well to others, is satisfied with his life. Performs up to mental and physical capacity and is able to function well in most areas.

Mental defectiveness is present requiring institutional training or custodial care that is not provided.

Child has disease which endangers public health; no measures are taken for isolation or treatment. Other serious health conditions or handicaps are present for which proper care is not provided.

retardation severely limits functioning, but special training, such as special class, is received.

Child not retarded but performs well below capacity.

Chronic or major physical disease or handicap is present; receives some treatment, but permits minimal functioning.

Diseases or handicaps, if present, are receiving appropriate care with resulting favorable adjustment.

Role Performance:

As Child: There is violent, destructive, or assaultive behavior against family members.

As Pupil: Excessive truancy, disruptiveness, incorrigibility, property destruction necessitates intervention. Other infringements of school regulations result in suspension, expulsion, etc.

As Peer: Participates with others in delinquent acts. Inability to relate to peers suggests severe emotional disturbance. Is often involved in severe conflicts with peers.

Role Performance:

As Child: Gets along poorly with parents and siblings, rarely performs household or other duties expected of him.

As Pupil: Acting-out or withdrawn behavior is of less serious nature. Attendance is not regular but no action is taken. School work is poor. There is little positive feeling toward school.

As Peer: Has few friends; is in frequent conflict with peers; associates with groups whose behavior is not acceptable to immediate community.

Role Performance:

As Child: There are close ties to family members. Continuously participates in household duties and family life.

As Pupil: Attends regularly; school work approximates ability; there is positive attitude toward school. Acting out is limited to occasional pranks.

As Peer: Is well liked; has friends; participates satisfactorily in peer groups.

C. CARE AND TRAINING OF CHILDREN

1. Physical Care

Inadequate	Marginal	Adequate
Supply and care of clothes, cleanliness, diet, and health care for children is	Children do not receive proper diet, their sleep schedule is irregular and	Children's diet is nutritious; provisions are made for sufficient sleep and exercise.

seriously deficient, endangers their health or threatens adjustment in school and acceptance in peer groups. Vermin is a serious health or social handicap. (Above is so serious that intervention is warranted.)

insufficient for their needs. Sleeping quarters are crowded, parents are indifferent and lax in providing suitable exercise or recreational outlets for children. Clothing is in short supply, poorly maintained--personal hygiene neglected.

Children have suitable clothes, adequate sleeping space, and are kept clean. Health needs (preventive and remedial) are looked after promptly and appropriately.

2. Training Methods and Emotional Care

Inadequate

Affection is rarely shown to children; there is marked indifference or obvious rejection. Parents have pathological tie to children, use them as pawns. Physical and emotional cruelty is present. (Above is so serious that intervention is warranted.)

Parents' behavior standards are so deviant from wider community that children are encouraged toward anti-social acts.

Physical punishment is overly severe or inappropriate. There is extreme lack of discipline. There is inconsistency of methods in one parent or between parents, limits are not enforced, strong disagreement exists between parents on training. Approval is shown rarely or not at all. (Above directly contributes to delinquent behavior or otherwise puts children in danger.)

Marginal

Little affection is shown to children; parents are usually indifferent to or reject children, or are overly permissive. Children have little sense of emotional security. (Above is not of imminent danger to children.)

Parents' behavior standards are in many respects somewhat deviant from community, or there is a lack of standards, or parents expect too much or too little maturity.

Parents are overly rigid, over-permissive, indifferent. Physical punishment, swearing occurs. Discipline is not appropriate to behavior. Approval of good conduct is rare. Parents are inconsistent, often do not enforce limits, disagree with each other over exercise of discipline, do not share task of training. Parents show favoritism. (Above is potential rather than actual danger)

Adequate

Parents show steady affection for children, provide atmosphere of emotional warmth, sense of belonging.

Parents' ideas of how children should behave are generally those acceptable to the community. Standards of behavior are appropriate to age level.

Methods used are usually appropriate to behavior. Approval of good conduct is often shown. Parents are fairly consistent in exercising discipline, enforce limits set, agree with each other in exercising discipline, share job of training children.

D.   SOCIAL ACTIVITIES

    1.   Informal Associations

Inadequate	Marginal	Adequate
Conflict with relatives, neighbors, friends results in physical violence or illegal activities. Persons as above are such a disturbing and discordant influence on family as to endanger welfare of children. Friends participate in perpetrating delinquent antisocial acts.	There are broken, discordant, or indifferent relationships with relatives, squabbles with neighbors. Family members have few or no social outlets with friends or have friends whose influence leads to dubious social consequences (drunken sprees, consumption of drugs, destruction of property, children left alone, etc.)	Majority of relationships with relatives and friends are pleasant and satisfying. Amicable relationships maintained with neighbors. Family members have social outlets, appropriate to stage of family development, providing recreational and interpersonal satisfactions, sense of identification with larger groups, and necessary socialization experiences for children. Marital partners agree on how leisure time is to be spent.

    2.   Formal Associations

       Rate N. A. if there are no formal associations and respondents have no opinions, or only neutral attitudes, about formal associations. Where there is a need to belong to a formal association and a refusal to do so, the rating must be less than adequate. If negative views are expressed but no formal associations are in evidence, rate this sub-category but not below "marginal."

       Belonging to one organization, such as a labor union, does not necessarily qualify for an "adequate" rating. Into your judgment here must enter considerations on understanding the nature of organization, quality of participation, and general attitude towards the organization.

       Church membership alone does not qualify for a rating in this sub-category; however, being active in a church sponsored group or club does.

Inadequate	Marginal	Adequate
There is membership in formal groups perpetrating antisocial acts. Behavior in organized group is so destructive or disruptive that intervention is necessary.	Family feels socially alone and unable to improve social status. In contrast to other families in the community, family members belong to no organized groups.	Family members, where appropriate, belong to some clubs, organizations, unions, etc., participate in some activities and derive satisfaction from belonging. Some members are active in groups which lend support to community betterment.

E. ECONOMIC PRACTICES

1. Source and Amount of Income

If family is headed by an O. W. mother who lives with her parents or other members of her extended family and is completely dependent upon them economically, the family income is rated. If the O. W. mother subsists on her own income (could be ADC grant), even if she lives with her family, her income is rated independently of others. If part of the O. W. mother's income is her own, and part from her family, the focus is still on the adequacy of funds as it pertains to the O. W. mother and her children. In this instance, the income from her family may be seen as coming from an outside source, such as a pension, insurance etc.

Inadequate	Marginal	Adequate
Amount of income is so low or unstable that basic necessities are not provided for family members.	Amount of income is marginal or unstable, barely meets family needs.	Family is financially sufficiently independent to afford a few luxuries or savings, is fairly well satisfied with economic status, and is working toward greater financial security.
Family is frequently deprived of source of income because of failure of able-bodied family members to support. Income from Public Assistance is obtained through fraudulent means. Income is derived from theft, forgery, etc.	Income is derived from general relief or Public Assistance. Children in home, though of working age and not in school, are not employed or contributing to family income. Family is dissatisfied with amount of income.	Income is derived from work of family members, or from sources such as pensions, insurances, rent, support payments, etc., but money is not from public welfare funds.

2. Job Situation

Applies only to family members contributing substantially to support of family. If the unmarried mother is not employed because she has to care for her children, always rate N. A. Treat temporary or seasonal lay-offs (as in construction business) as if wage earner were employed.

Inadequate	Marginal	Adequate
Law-breaking behavior is exhibited on job, such as fraud, embezzlement, robbery, physical violence to co-workers.	There are frequent changes of job, unsteady work patterns; the employee works less than full time, job is below his capacity. There are poor relations with employer and co-workers and dissatisfaction with job.	Works regularly at full time job, seeks improvement if not fully satisfied, changes jobs only when it is unavoidable due to economic or other circumstances, or for improvement. Job is suitable for capabilities; worker maintains harmonious relations
Able-bodied man unwilling to obtain employment.		

with employer and co-
workers, and has
positive feeling toward
job.

3. Use of Money

Inadequate	Marginal	Adequate
Severe conflict over control of income endangers children's welfare. Budgeting and money management are so poor that basic necessities are not provided. Excessive debt results in legal action.	Disagreement over control of income leads to conflict or dissatisfaction among family members. Family is unable to live within budget, money management is poor, luxuries take precedence over basic necessities, there is impulsive spending. (Above do not seriously endanger family's welfare.)	Money is spent on the basis of agreement that such is responsibility of one or more members of family. Family budgets income; money management is carried out with realistic regard to basic necessities. Debts are manageable and planned for in budget.

F. HOME AND HOUSEHOLD PRACTICES

1. Physical Facilities

Inadequate	Marginal	Adequate
Property is in deteriorated condition, kept in very poor state of repair. Facilities for sleeping, washing, sanitation, heat, water, refrigeration, or cooking are so inadequate as to be an actual threat to the physical and emotional welfare of family members, particularly children, and necessitate intervention by health or other authorities. Homes and stores along street are in advanced state of deterioration. Trash, garbage, abandoned cars, various junk	Property is deteriorating and in need of repair, or sufficient space is not available. There is absence or inadequacy of basic household equipment. (Above potentially harmful to welfare of children.) Homes and stores along streets are in poor state of repair. Streets are poorly maintained; there are not enough play areas for children, who either have to play on sidewalks or go a great distance to a park or playground. Heavy automobile traffic makes it potentially dangerous for children	Property is kept in good condition; there is sufficient space for family members. Necessary household equipment is available and in good working order. Family members are satisfied and pleased with their home. Streets and sidewalks are kept clean and in good condition. There is sufficient illumination, and streets are "safe" to walk on, both day and night. Play and recreational areas for children are available within short walking distance. Neighborhood usually designated as

objects are scattered along streets and vacant lots, create a health hazard to the residents. Area is not considered "safe" after dark. Among loiterers on street and in doorways one can identify "skid-row" elements such as alcoholics, dope addicts, hustlers, etc. There are no play areas for youngsters, or if such exist, they are dangerous to the welfare of children.

to cross street or play on sidewalks. A home along a busy main thoroughfare, which may be satisfactory for adults, constitutes a potential danger area for young children. Home in close proximity to factories which create noise and pollute the air.

"residential" and consists mainly of dwelling units in good state of repair and upkeep.

2. Housekeeping Standards

Inadequate	Marginal	Adequate
Home is maintained in such a dirty and unsanitary condition, meals are so irregular, diet is so inadequate as to constitute an actual hazard to physical well being of family members. Vermin or rats present serious health hazard.	Home is in disorder, meals are irregular, diet is poorly planned, making a potential hazard to physical welfare of family members.	Home is maintained in a condition conducive to good health, hygiene, and a sense of orderliness. Meals are served regularly, diet is well balanced and nutritious. Attention is paid to making home attractive and pleasant to family members.

G. HEALTH CONDITIONS AND PRACTICES

1. Health Conditions

Mental illness and maladjustment is not to be considered here, but is evaluated under Individual Behavior and Adjustment.

Inadequate	Marginal	Adequate
Presence of communicable disease endangers public health; patient is not isolated or properly treated. Major or chronic disease or handicap so severely limits person's functioning within and outside the home that	Disease, chronic illness, or handicaps limit person's functioning inside and outside home, but it constitutes no actual threat to family welfare.	Physical health of family members is such that they are able to function satisfactorily in their various roles. Good health, including condition of teeth, is generally apparent.

there is an actual
threat to family
welfare, particularly
the care children are
receiving.

2. Health Practices

Inadequate	Marginal	Adequate
Proper treatment or quarantine is not secured for diseases endangering life of person and/or public health. Parents neglect or refuse to provide medical or other remedial care for health and well-being of children. Disease prevention practices (sanitation, diet, etc.) are not followed. Conditions are so poor that physical neglect of children is involved.	There is refusal or failure to get or continue medical care for minor ailments. Medical instructions are disregarded or not followed consistently. Disease prevention practices are not generally followed, but health of family members is not seriously endangered.	Concern is shown about ill health or handicaps, medical care is promptly sought when needed, medical instructions are followed. Disease prevention and dental hygiene practices are observed.

H.   RELATIONSHIP TO SOCIAL WORKER

Rate N. A. unless there is a professional relationship of significance
between an intervention worker and family life.

1.   Attitude Towards Worker

Inadequate	Marginal	Adequate
There is physical violence or verbal assault and other types of threatening or insulting behavior.	Worker is met with suspicion, resentment, or defensiveness on part of family, or marked indifference.	Worker is received with friendliness or affective neutrality, with readiness to consider family problems in relation to services offered.

2.   Use of Worker

Inadequate	Marginal	Adequate
There is refusal to talk with worker when the basis of community	Client is reluctant to to engage in social work relationship and	Client shows willingness to engage in a positive social work

concern is such that the worker has a right to stay in the situation. There is absolute refusal to acknowledge any problems. Deceptive and fraudulent behavior is shown toward worker.

to recognize and/or deal with problems which face him and his family. There is manipulative use of worker.

relationship, and to work towards enhancing or improving family's social functioning. Client freely calls on worker in pursuit of this goal.

I. USE OF COMMUNITY RESOURCES

If family has no knowledge of any health, social, and recreational resources, a "near adequate" rating, at best, can be given.

The expression of a critical opinion about any resource when that resource has shortcomings does not call for a negative rating.

If respondent has no associations with social and recreational agencies, rate N. A. If there is a need for using a community resource but a refusal to do so, a less than "adequate" rating must be assigned. If respondent has no connections with, or present need for using a community resource but expresses a negative opinion (e. g. , "I heard so many terrible things about relief that I would starve first before going to them for help. ") rating may be lower than "adequate" but cannot be below "marginal. "

1.   School

Rate parents' attitude towards schools and education, even if all children are of pre-school age.

Inadequate	Marginal	Adequate
Parents are extremely hostile to school, encourage or abet consistent truancy, are antagonistic to school personnel, refuse to cooperate when this is made necessary by the seriousness of community concern. Children have extremely negative attitude toward school, are excessively truant without excuse, are very disruptive, destroy school property, commit other infringements of school regulations demanding intervention.	Parents place little value on education, take little interest in children's school activities, are lax in enforcing attendance, are uncooperative with school in plans for children. Children have negative attitude toward school, truant rather frequently, are a disruptive or disturbing influence, do poor school work (but not sufficiently serious to warrant intervention).	Parents value education for their children, facilitate regular school attendance, are cooperative with school personnel when joint planning is indicated. Children value school, attend regularly, are not behavior problems, achieve according to capacity.

2. Church

Check in the "adequate" to "marginal" range only if family member(s) is participating in church activities. If there are no church ties, or only nominal church membership, check N. A. "Inadequate" may, however, be checked regardless of whether family has church ties.

Inadequate	Marginal	Adequate
Law violations are directed against church, such as robbery, destruction of property, committing nuisances, vandalism, etc. Instill hostile attitudes in children toward religion. Serious religious conflict between parents has negative effect upon children.	Family members are a disruptive influence in a church group. There is a little satisfaction from church affiliation; there is conflict among family members about church attendance or participation in church sponsored activities.	Attend church fairly regularly, whenever possible; derive personal satisfaction from church ties.

3. Health Resources

If private doctors or dentists are used, they are viewed and rated the same as any other health resource. Mental health resources are to be covered under L 4., Social Agencies.

Inadequate	Marginal	Adequate
Hostility or bitterness or apathy toward available health resources are so great that serious health problems of family members do not receive medical attention. Health needs of parents, which prevent them from caring for children, are not met.	Family regards health resources with suspicion, hostility, or resentment. Agencies are used unconstructively, appointments are missed, follow-through is lacking, medical advice is not followed, but not to the extent of seriously endangering welfare of family members.	Family has positive attitude toward health agencies and resources; available facilities are used promptly when need arises, appointments are kept, medical advice is followed.

4. Social Agencies

Includes correctional services, housing authority, employment agencies, welfare agencies, mental health and social adjustment services. If client is not using social agencies, and has no need to do so, rate N. A.

Inadequate	Marginal	Adequate
There is extreme hostility to social agencies leading to behavior such as assault, robbery, or destruction of property, fraud, etc. There is refusal to accept agency services where this has been ordered by law or is necessary because of community concern.	Attitude toward agencies is marked by hostility, resentment, defensiveness, apathy, etc. Agencies are used unconstructively-- family is not cooperative, or is apathetic, or overly demanding, etc.	Attitude toward agencies is positive. Family utilizes agencies appropriately for improvement of family life or for meeting needs of individual members, is cooperative in working on joint plans.

5. Recreational Agencies

Refers only to publicly sponsored facilities. Participation in commercial enterprises, like bowling alleys, amusement parks, dance-clubs, etc., will be rated under D. Social Activities.

Inadequate	Marginal	Adequate
Hostility toward recreational agencies leads to assault, robbery, destruction of property, etc. Parents prevent children from using organized recreational facilities.	Children seldom use recreational facilities such as playgrounds, etc. If use is made, behavior is characterized by disruptiveness, noncooperation, etc.	Family members, particularly children, make use of available recreational resources according to age and interest; resources and services provide satisfaction and necessary socialization experience for children.

(IV. 5.)   The Rating Procedure

Rating or coding is a process used when one wishes to reduce qualitative or descriptive data to a quantitative (nominal, ordinal, or interval) format.   Rating requires the application of judgment; it is generally guided by instructions or guidelines which in our case are quite detailed, for the more specific the instructions the less room there is for idiosyncratic judgment on the part of the rater.   Although we have attempted to minimize the introduction of subjective considerations, it is obvious that they cannot be completely eliminated.   To rate family functioning one must compare a situation described in the Profile of Family Functioning with the criteria, which are descriptions at a higher level of abstraction.   A certain amount of subjective judgment enters into the making of every comparison because there is usually some discrepancy between the descriptive level and that of the criterion.

Before rating is undertaken the researcher must accept the premise that it is a theoretically justified method.   The rater must understand the conceptual organization of the material because the coding of complex narrative data, such as we have here, frequently necessitates a mental reordering of content scattered in overlapping categories.   It can be assumed that knowledge of the behavioral sciences is helpful in coding, but whether a graduate education makes a better coder is a moot question.   This writer with rather extensive experience has found that coders with both undergraduate and graduate training have performed with seemingly comparable results.

The following guidelines should be helpful in rating a Profile of Family Functioning:

(1)   As a first step the coder will find it helpful to keep in mind the continuum, shown below, for scoring sub-categories and main categories of social functioning.

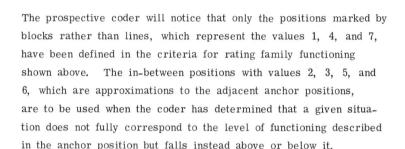

The prospective coder will notice that only the positions marked by
blocks rather than lines, which represent the values 1, 4, and 7,
have been defined in the criteria for rating family functioning
shown above.   The in-between positions with values 2, 3, 5, and
6, which are approximations to the adjacent anchor positions,
are to be used when the coder has determined that a given situation does not fully correspond to the level of functioning described
in the anchor position but falls instead above or below it.

     (2) The coder should read over the criteria for rating
family functioning and study carefully the general criteria.   The
specific criteria should be examined closely at the time the case
is being rated.

     (3) The Profile of Family Functioning should now be read
in its entirety.   For purposes of rating, a grasp of the entire
family picture is necessary, because even the best organized
protocol will have some information missing or incompletely
covered under the proper heading and placed elsewhere.   The
coder who has studied the entire case will use this information
appropriately and will also be aware of the extent to which information is completely missing from the Profile.   The reading at this
point should cover only the beginning situation or first Profile.
This will help avoid confusion in the mind of the coder regarding
different temporal stages in family functioning.

     (4) The next step calls for a reading and subsequent rating
of the Profile, sub-category by sub-category and area (or main
category) by area.   Each group of sub-categories making up an
area is rated before coding the area as a whole.   Ratings are

entered in the appropriate column on the code sheet shown on the
next page. A rating will take one of three forms: A substantive
or numerical area or sub-category rating in the form of a whole
number between 1 and 7; an N. K. or "not known" because the information under a given heading is missing; and an N. A. or "not
applicable, " whenever information under a given heading is irrelevant. The latter would include the sub-category "sibling relationships" when there is only one child, or the sub-category "job
situation" if no one in the family is employed.

(5) The area or main category scores are a composite of
the sub-category ratings. The former require a judgmental weighting of the latter, rather than a statistical procedure such as com-
puting the mean or mode. The numerical values of sub-categories
limit the range within which area scores can be assigned. In
other words, if sub-category ratings are all 4's and 5's, the area
score cannot be 3 or 6 but must be either 4 or 5. The value of
the final score depends upon which sub-categories are dominant in
describing the characteristics of the family's functioning within the
total area. For instance, Care and Training of Children which is
characterized by poor "training and emotional care" (because of
inconsistent discipline, cruelty, and preferential treatment of one
child) but adequate "physical care" should be assigned a low area
score. The coder will have to judge whether the high rating in
"physical care" should result in a main category score slightly
higher than the rating for "training and emotional care. " The area
score might be upgraded if the coder had evidence that the good
"physical care" helped reduce the harm done by inferior training
and emotional care.

(6) The score for Individual Behavior and Adjustment is
also a composite, and the weighting of scores of family members
to be rated takes into account their influence upon family life. The
score weight for a separated father who visits the family on occasion is lower than that of a mother in the home. Similarly, a
baby in the crib is given a lower weight than a teenager who takes
an active part in family life. Separate ratings are given for the

father, mother, older children (10 years and over), and younger children (under 10 years). Coders may not wish to group children into two collective categories but rate each of them separately. If this is done, separate scores for each child according to age can be entered into their respective categories.

(7) After rating the beginning situation the coder can undertake the rating of the second Profile, if there is indeed a second one. A cross-sectional study may involve only a single evaluation of family functioning whereas dynamic studies, either of the before-after or panel type, would have two or more Profiles, the second of which would cover a designated time period following the beginning situation. Since the second (or subsequent) Profile was written with reference to changes occurring since the beginning situation, the rating must also be done in such a fashion. To do this the coder who scores the after situation must familiarize himself with the contents and the scores of the beginning Profile. Only after such preparation will he proceed, as he did in the first coding, by reading the narrative in the later Profile and assigning ratings according to the level of functioning criteria. A separate score sheet, identical with the first one, will be used with the appropriate ordinal Profile number checked.

(8) Movement is the numerical difference between scores of a given Profile and those of a later one, arrived at by simply subtracting scores and entering the sum in the movement score sheet shown below. Three types of movement may be differentiated: positive, zero, and negative. Positive and negative movement can range from 1 to 6, the latter representing a situation where the change is from a score of 1 (inadequate) to 7 (adequate) or the converse.

(9) The heuristic device of graphing the Profile of Family Functioning may be decided upon if the instrument is to be given clinical use. One chart would be employed for graphing the beginning and after (or several subsequent) situations; a second one would be used for showing movement, and an example of this will follow the case presentation below. Groups of cases can also be

represented pictorially, with the graph being based on mean scores and standard deviations which are marked off--by means of different colors or broken and straight lines--at intervals on both sides of each graph.

The following presentation of an actual case should help clarify the foregoing instructions and guidelines for profiling and rating. In recent years the St. Paul Scale of Family Functioning has been used rather extensively to study relatively "normal" families, and this case may be said to fall under this heading. It may be recalled that the instrument was developed originally to assess the social functioning of disorganized families, and the case example presented in the first manual on measurement[16] belonged to that category. However, this case study is more typical of the "normal" type of family, the kind researched in the Family Life Improvement Project, for instance, [17] than the type of disorganized family studied by the St. Paul Family Centered Project or the Chemung County Study. [18]

The case presented below constitutes a study of change by virtue of the fact that two separate Profiles are shown, describing social functioning over an 18 month period. For easier comparison the beginning and after situation are juxtaposed on the same page, rather than on separate pages as recommended in the instructions. The family described here has been receiving professional social work services for child behavior and marital problems. Movement in family functioning, as the reader will notice, coincides with positive changes in treatment. However, the Profile writer does not assume any cause and effect relationship between service and movement in social functioning. On the contrary, a careful reading of the Profile will show that many important changes were due to circumstances beyond the reach of the professional intervener, such as the improved employment situation resulting from the establishment of a new family business. Yet, other positive changes, particularly in the child rearing process, might be traced more directly to the activities of the social worker.

This case study of the Z. family is, in fact, a good

illustration of the complex inter-relationship between intervention
programs on the one hand, and change in family functioning on
the other.   Efforts aimed at providing something approximating a
casual nexus must be devoted to meeting such requirements of
experimental design building as hypothesizing the specific changes
anticipated as a result of services and setting up one or more
matched control groups to check the effects of nonexperimental
variables on family functioning.

The Z. family, as both the narrative and the score Profile
will show, is not particularly problematic.   Social functioning is
above the marginal coordinate defined as the level at which behavior may be said to be potentially threatening to the welfare of
family members or the community.   On the other hand, there are
several areas and sub-areas where functioning is near marginal,
denoting dissatisfactions, stresses, and strains in family life.
Adequate or near adequate functioning in the after situation denotes
concrete though not spectacular improvement over an 18 month
period.   The essential dynamic of the Z.'s functioning is in the
narrative, not the score Profile.   The latter represents--as does
all quantitative research--a form of data reduction which makes
the loss of some content inevitable.   The conceptual organization
of scores, nonetheless, makes the numerical Profile quite meaningful without a spelling out of the content of areas and sub-categories.
But while the numerical or graphic family Profile may have some
clinical uses, its essential value resides in its potential for making
the study of family functioning a scientific enterprise in which
hypotheses can be tested and theories developed.

(IV. 5.) The Z. Family as an Example of Profiling and

Rating Family Functioning

A. FAMILY RELATIONSHIPS AND UNITY

1. Marital Relationship

a. History

The young couple met at a fraternity party at an eastern
state university when Mrs. Z. was 19 and Mr. Z. was 23 and in
service.   There was no formal engagement for there was very
little time between the initial meeting and their marriage.   He saw
her during his brief leave, wrote to her from his base, and pro-
posed after a few letters.   Mrs. Z. was impressed by his service
affiliation and officer's rank (second lieutenant), by his age, and by
his extroverted manner and competence as master of ceremonies
at the fraternity dance.   Mr. Z. liked her outgoing and decisive
personality and the easy popularity she seemed to enjoy.   Mr. Z.'s
father (his mother had died when he was eight) who was a store-
keeper in a small town in Delaware was glad he found a Jewish
bride.   Mrs. Z. had had a promiscuous past for which she had
received therapy.   Her father, afraid that she was known to be
"fast" in their community, a medium-sized city in New Jersey,
and therefore unacceptable to most of the families there, advised
her to marry this out-of-town boy and she took his advice.   They
arranged a military wedding near his base in Texas.

The Z.'s set up housekeeping in a small apartment off
base, far from family and in a part of the country which was new
and strange to them.   Mr. Z. was gone on training flights for
long periods of time, leaving his young wife alone with a few
other army wives for company.   They decided to have a child as
quickly as possible.   Shortly after their first child, a boy, was
born, Mr. Z. was discharged from the service.   Returning to his
hometown, Mr. Z. found a job in a nearby city as radio announcer,
a position for which he had been trained.   But another child was
on its way, and he found the pay meager with little chance of ad-
vancement.   They moved, then, to her hometown, which was larger
and where employment seemed a little more promising.

There followed a period of a year in which Mr. Z. tried to
sell insurance.   But the personality difficulties which his wife had
first observed in Texas--passivity, lethargy, general lack of self
discipline and aggressiveness--hindered him.   He would often become depressed and sit idly at home while weeks drifted by and
income ceased.   Increasingly, Mrs. Z. found herself making the
decisions about housing, purchases, payment or deferment of bills.
Her father told her that she would have to take over and be the
decisive one in the family.   It was during this period, in fact,
that Mrs. Z. became much closer to her father, using him both
as a confidant to whom she could complain about her husband and
an advisor who could help her manage the household.   Mr. Z., on
the other hand, found in his father-in-law the father he had never
had, for he had been reared by an aunt.   The father-in-law's protection and advice were actively sought by Mr. Z., while at the
same time he expressed the desire to impress him by making a
great deal of money in the insurance business.

During this period they saw few people besides family.
Mr. Z.'s father had remarried but Mr. Z. refused to have anything to do with his stepmother.   Mrs. Z. intervened, convinced
her husband that they should drive down with the children and visit
over the weekend, and, on the pretext of introducing the boys to
their grandmother, helped her husband accept the new family member.   They often visited with Mrs. Z.'s parents (the L.'s) and extended family but did not see many of the friends Mrs. Z. had
made as a teen-ager.

From the beginning the couple's sexual patterns had been
problematic.   Mr. Z. was upset about his wife's lack of response.
Learning that she had had intimacies before marriage, he felt her
apparent coldness was a reaction to him.   Mrs. Z., however, insisted that sexual relationships had never been satisfying for her.
After the two boys were born in quick succession, they used a
diaphragm to thwart further conception.   Mrs. Z. often expressed
the wish that they had waited before having children.

On the whole, Mr. Z. gave evidence of being content with

his family.   He seemed pleased with the home and the routine and
ties it provided.   Mrs. Z. , on the other hand, resented the amount
of initiative she had to take in financial matters and her husband's
lack of help in keeping house or caring for children.   She was embarrassed at their shabby apartment and her lack of clothing and
distressed over her husband's failure to make a living.   In her
teens when she had not responded in her first sexual encounters
there had been little anxiety, but now she was upset by her apparent frigidity.

The first child had come within the first year of marriage,
and Mrs. Z. had been very pleased by the pregnancy which set her
apart from her young friends.   On a short trip home from Texas
she had preened herself in the eyes of family and friends.   The
arrival of the child, however, found her unprepared for the responsibility and demands it brought.   Her mother (Mrs. L.) flew
down to help her but, indecisive and unwell, she proved to be of
little help.   The baby had long periods of crying which tired the
young mother, but Mr. Z. did not realize that he could or should
be of help and spent most of the leave (which had been arranged
to coincide with the birth) watching television.   The pattern of
noninvolvement persisted.   Mrs. Z. retained responsibility for
child care even at times of illness or when her husband was idle,
and she was very resentful of this.

Mr. Z. was very proud of his son at birth but became less
interested in him as he grew older.   Essentially the same could
be said for the second child.   Mrs. Z. found them a source of
pride but also seemed worn out from trying to cope with them.

A. 1. b. Present Functioning

Mr. and Mrs. Z. enjoy
similar recreational activities
(baseball, bowling) and like the
same types of movies and television programs.   They both
would enjoy active memberships

A. 1. b. Present Functioning

Some eighteen months later
there is less tension in the household, probably a result of Mr. Z. 's
new job.   No longer on his own
in a selling position, he now
works for his father-in-law in

in social and fraternal organizations and wish they had more
leisure time to pursue these.

Mrs. Z. is a strong willed,
quick tempered, decisive woman while Mr. Z. is a socia-
ble, eager to please, dependent
man with a fund of jokes and
tall tales. Mrs. Z. indicates
that she would like to make
fewer of the family's financial
decisions and is resentful of
being pushed into the dominant
position. Mr. Z., who has a
tendency to become depressed
and then immobile, retreats
from her anger when she "blows
up" and defends himself by becoming silent or preoccupied.
He covers up for inadequacies
by lying and finds himself unable
to talk out their marital difficulties.

Presently, Mr. Z. is em-
ployed selling house-to-house
for a national firm, but he is
not happy with the job or his
performance. Although he
seems to have a salesman's
outgoing personality and does
well in initial contacts, his
selling record is erratic, he
does not win sales contests,
he has not been promoted to
district manager, and, most

a newly bought suburban liquor
store. With a closely super-
vised structure of hours and
tasks and assured clients,
there has been no recurrence
of depression. Thus, one of
the main triggers to Mrs. Z.'s
spells of vocal anger has been
removed.

Mrs. Z. continues to make
most of the household decisions,
but she is acknowledging now
that she enjoys doing it. Mr. Z.,
however, was the moving force
in planning their first vacation
this summer. He chose the
site (Shenandoah Forest), decided to rent a camper, and
mapped out their route. Mr. Z.
is attempting to help with the
children and chores, sometimes
disposing of the garbage, drying
dishes, bathing the children when
his time allows. It is still difficult for him to acknowledge
or talk out marital problems,
and he continues to retreat
from direct conversations
about this with his wife.
Mrs. Z. is less unhappy
about caring for the house
now that Mr. Z. is working
under structured circumstances. The home is usually
clean and, although not tidy

important, his take-home pay fluctuates widely from week to week. He has never attained his goal of becoming successful by making a great deal of money.

The people they see are those who come to the occasional club meetings the Z.'s attend and the bi-monthly bowling league which is mandatory for firm members. Mrs. Z. is embarrassed by her small house and does not invite her old friends to her home. She cannot pay a sitter but does take off a few times a month to play mah jongg when her mother comes to relieve her. At these times Mrs. L. usually cleans the house--especially the kitchen--which is never kept clean. Their main form of socializing is visiting the L.'s three or four times a week. There are a number of family members--sisters, aunts, and cousins--with professional or successful business positions to whom the Z.'s feel inferior. They do not cease taking part in family activities on this account, however. The family's long range goal is to make enough money to buy a larger house, to be as finan-

at all times, it no longer offends her mother.

Mrs. Z. is attempting to become less involved with her own extended family, especially her father, although this is difficult because the job situation forces them into close contact. The Z.'s decided to buy furniture for the living room without prior consultation with the L.'s, and the wife is trying to stop her habit of complaining to them about her husband. The Z.'s have decided to limit their visits with the L.'s to Sunday. The wife has discouraged unexpected visits by her parents by leaving the house to do chores when they dropped by. Increasingly, the Z.'s are attemping to create a social group of peers. She has invited old friends with husbands to dinner twice in the last two months (she explains that they now have a dining room set) and her sewing club is planning to have a party in their recreation room next week.

Mr. Z. still has little confidence in himself. The liquor store had trouble with the police when he unintentionally sold beer to a minor and cially successful and secure as other members of their family and social class.

As was mentioned before, Mrs. Z. decides how the weekly check is to be handled, when to pay debts, what purchases to make. She is not reconciled to this responsibility and has told her husband so. She makes the decisions about child care, securing medical services, and their occasional social activities. Buying the house was a joint decision, with Mrs. Z. taking the lead and her father supporting their decision. The second car was also a joint purchase, but without the in-laws consent. The Z.'s felt there should be another car to use during the day when their first one is needed for selling. On the whole, though, whenever they are faced with a difficult decision, Mrs. Z. takes the initiative after asking her father for advice.

While Mr. Z. supports the family, he relies upon his wife to keep the sales accounts and to help him pack merchandise to fill the orders. A number of nights a week must be devoted to putting orders together and checking the accounts.

then repeated the same offense a few weeks later. His father-in-law reprimanded him severely, for it meant losing their license for a short time. Mr. L. has forbidden him to make policy decisions; Mrs. Z. feels this is just as well since she questions his ability to do so. On the other hand, customers ask for Mr. Z. if Mr. L. is in the store, for they enjoy his friendly manner. Mr. L. has attempted to give him credit for this popularity, which is essential if the store is to survive.

In the beginning, Mrs. Z. was involved in the new business, staying in the store late in the evenings while her husband made deliveries, a service they hoped would increase business. (Mrs. L. was too ill to help and Mr. L. had another job at that time, trusting Mr. Z. to be the store's manager.) But Mrs. Z. deeply resented this demand upon her at a time when her children were at home and had to eat supper. Sometimes the children were left alone to feed themselves if a sitter were unavailable. This practice

Mrs. Z. has, at times, helped her husband by delivering the goods, thus freeing him to do more selling. But through all these acts of co-operation runs a thread of anger which is exhibited in eruptions of shouting and arguments whenever she considers too much time is being taken in this fashion to the detriment of the children or the running of the household. She feels too many tasks are allotted to her and that her husband does not carry responsibility for enough areas.

Their sexual adjustment stands as described under History; he is defensive and feels he is a failure while she is anxious and worried about her lack of response.

was discontinued when Mr. L.'s other job was terminated, and the two men began caring for the store together.

The Z.'s seem to have found a partial solution to their sexual problems. They have found that Mrs. Z. can respond if there is prolonged foreplay and special positions are used. However, Mrs. Z. feels somewhat guilty about this, and it is doubtful that this can long satisfy Mr. Z.'s determination to prove his ability with her.

A. 2. Relationship Between Parents and Children

There is not much display of affection between parents and children. The mother directs their home activities with sharp commands and then sends them out to play in the neighborhood. The husband spends almost no time with them. Both parents shout and slap when discipline is needed. Mr. Z. will often ignore them until

A. 2. Relationship Between Parents and Children

Mr. Z. is spending more time caring for the children-- bathing them in the evenings and getting Sunday morning breakfast for them. Mrs. Z. has enrolled them at the Jewish Center now that their salary can cover the expense and is happy to have them both taking swimming lessons. But essentially the parents

he bursts out with angry
shouts, after which he will
withdraw.

Mrs. Z. has been con-
cerned about their summer activities. She has gotten the
oldest boy in a Little League
and sends both of them to the
local playground program.
She voices disappointment at
being unable to pay the membership fee at the Jewish
Center nearby, where the
children could learn to swim.

The parents seem to
favor the younger child, Danial,
over the older one, Jonathan,
by disciplining him less and requiring fewer tasks of him.
The older one is frequently
told that "he is old enough to
know better. " While there is
no outright rejection, the
mother frequently exhibits annoyance and the father ha-
bitually displays indifference
to them.

have not altered their pattern
of indifference and noncommuni-
cation, and there is still little
outward show of emotional
warmth. Discipline is still
achieved by sudden reprimands,
yells, and slaps.

Mrs. Z. is attempting to
change her apparent favoring
of the younger child. She is
trying to be less severe in
disciplining Jonathan and com-
mending him upon the small
progress he makes in school.

A. 3. Relationship Among
      Children

The two children, Jonathan
and Danial, feel strongly that
they have a common origin.
When his Grandmother pre-
sents him with candy, Jonathan
always asks whether she brought

A. 3. Relationship Among
      Children

Jonathan, on the swim
team, has told Danial that,
when he grows a little and
becomes a stronger swimmer,
he can join too. He continues
to bully him at home, however,

some for Danial too. Danial
follows Jonathan around on
his adventures in the neighborhood and boasts that his big
brother plays in the Little
League. Although Jonathan
attempts to "lose" his younger
brother, he goes to the playground program with him in
the summer and usually can
tell his mother where to find
the younger one.

Jonathan is jealous, how-
ever, of Danial's position as
"baby" in the family. Danial
receives what little show of
affection there is, and Jonathan
reacts by talking loudly, creat-
ing a disturbance at meals,
refusing to share toys with his
brother and sometimes bullying him.

refusing to share toys. But
he now allows him to enter his
room and has stopped making
each meal a battlefield.

A. 4. Family Solidarity

Although they have prob-
lems, the family presents a
fairly united front. The only
weakness in family solidarity
is Mrs. Z.'s involvement of
her father in family affairs,
often leading to the exclusion
of her husband in decision making (see also A. 1. b.). They
visit in-laws (the L.'s) many
times a week; the parents bowl
together twice a month; they

A. 4. Family Solidarity

No changes in the activity
patterns of the family, but
Mrs. Z. has been trying to
become less involved with
her family of origin and
has reduced the amount of
complaining to her father
about her husband (see also
A. 1. b.).

have meals together when
schedules permit; they attempt
to keep their home and grounds
in order.   Mrs. Z. entertained
for a visiting sister by inviting
the entire extended family to
her recreation room.   Twice
a year they take the children
by car to visit Mr. Z.'s
family 130 miles away.

The entire family usually
has Friday night supper with
Mrs. Z.'s parents, where her
father will recite prayers and
the mother will serve traditional dishes.   Lately Mrs. L.
has been unable to have them
all to dinner and so the children take turns being guests.
On hot days the Z.'s and the
L.'s go to the shore together;
in the autumn they have pic-
nics in the park.   On holidays
the extended family meets at
an aunt's large house for a
barbecue.

There is very little out-
ward show of emotional warmth
in this family.   Hugs and kisses
are reserved for few occasions
and generally given only to the
younger boy.   The grandparents
do not kiss the children when
they arrive and give only small
pecks on the cheek before bed-

time. When Mrs. Z.'s sister
arrived after an extended absence, the greetings were pleasant but did not indicate the state
of pleasure which the family members testified that they felt at the
reunion. It may be noted that the
L. family gives free rein to feelings of anger and frustration but
has difficulty indicating love,
pleasure, and joy. While the
grandparents see the children
often, they do not spend time
playing with them or taking
them places. After acknowledging them for a few minutes the
adults begin their own conversation, generally ignoring the children for the rest of the visit.
Mr. L. will often spend an entire
Sunday afternoon talking to his
daughter while excluding his
son-in-law as well as his own
wife.

Mr. and Mrs. Z. are avid television watchers, take a great interest
in spectator sports, and bowl at least
once a month. Mrs. Z. is interested
in modern novels which she likes to
discuss with her father. Neither parent is involved in community affairs
or politics. Religious observance is
restricted to the high holidays and
participation in sabbath and holiday
ritual at the home of the maternal
grandparents (see also D. 1.).

B. INDIVIDUAL BEHAVIOR AND ADJUSTMENT

   1. Parents

      a. History

(1) Mr. Z. 's parents were Jewish immigrants born in Russia who first settled in New York City and later came to Delaware for purposes of making a living. Born in 1939, Mr. Z. was an only child left motherless at the age of eight. He was raised by an aunt with three children of her own while his father ran a store in a nearby town. Mr. Z. always felt unwelcome in his aunt's home; he saw his father only for brief periods on Sunday afternoons when he visited him at the store.

The aunt's home was in a middle-class neighborhood. Her husband ran a small dry cleaning establishment; they managed on a tight budget. The aunt was active in Jewish affairs, and the children took part in Jewish center activities, which Mr. Z. also joined. The elder Mr. Z. centered all his interest in business and real estate investments which he managed to make over the years.

Mr. Z. attended an eastern seaboard state university, lived in a fraternity house, majored in dramatics. Well liked, he became something of a campus celebrity, officiating as disc jockey at many functions. On vacations he worked as short order cook at a luncheonette. After graduation he joined the Air Force, was trained as a navigator, married his wife when he was 23, approximately a year-and-a-half before separation from service.

(2) Mrs. Z. 's parents, U. S. born, were also Jewish of New Jersey origin. Both were high school graduates. There were four daughters in the family, with Mrs. Z. being the youngest, born in 1943.

There was always a great deal of conflict in Mrs. Z. 's parental home. Mr. L. felt superior to his wife, was autocratic in manner, and showed little respect or regard for family members. The L. 's had married originally when they were just out of high school because of an unwanted pregnancy, and both extended families were suspicious and unfriendly to each other. When Mrs. Z. was

born her mother worked in the family grocery, and a good deal of
Mrs. Z.'s childhood was spent in the store with her mother.   She
was ignored by the father who had wanted a son, and she was a
bother to her overworked mother.   Mrs. Z.'s older sisters took
over some of her care.   With the oldest she had an especially
close relationship, but the younger one was always jealous of her.
Her mother was always in poor health and finally gave up working
when Mrs. Z. was 12.   The parents often talked of separating or
of obtaining a divorce.   Although they did not regularly attend
religious services, they celebrated major holidays and took part
in Jewish Center activities.   Mr. L's greatest concern was to
make more money.   Since his children were female, he did not
plan to send them to college.

The family lived in a variety of apartments in lower-class
neighborhoods, close to their grocery which gave a small and irregular income.   Finally, they moved to a suburb, bought a store
there which gave them a more secure financial footing.   Their
social contacts were limited to the extended family.

When the oldest sister married and moved away, the first
of Mrs. Z.'s delinquent episodes occurred.   She was caught steal-
ing money and cigarettes to give to schoolboy acquaintances.   She
received therapy at the city Child Guidance Clinic for approximatel;
six months.   Although the therapists asked to see the parents, her
father refused.

While at high school where she did above average academic
work, she was involved in a number of love affairs.   Once more i1
therapy, the whole family became involved, the father now becoming concerned and attempting to spend time with her and to change
his attitudes.

One sister married a businessman and lives in the same
community; two married professionals and have moved to other
parts of the country.   All of them enjoy higher standards of living
than the Z. family.

Mrs. Z. attended a state college for a year before she mar
ried.   Her father, attempting to undo years of neglect, paid her

tuition, took her on trips, bought her a great deal of clothing. At school she took liberal arts courses, was interested in art, became an officer in a nonresident sorority. The only job she had before marriage was as checkout girl in a supermarket. As for hobbies, she knitted well, liked to bowl, and was good in organizing club activities.

B. 1. b.   Present Functioning:

(1) Mr. Z. is short, stocky, dark-haired with a pleasant smile. He likes to tell jokes and humorous stories; will become extremely quiet if overlooked. He tells tall tales about his selling adventures and achievements. He has had a number of accidents lately while selling and he enjoys telling of them in detail, dwelling on physical symptoms. He is interested in work, sports, latest sports statistics. A college graduate, he cannot discuss books or problems of the day with his professional relatives who believe he has no aptitude for abstract thinking.

Mr. Z. finds it difficult to work without outside direction and authority and becomes unable to move when things seem to be going badly. He feels himself unsuccessful in providing for his family and bristles at any imagined insult. He very openly relies upon his

B. 1. b.   Present Functioning:

(1) [Mr. Z.] There have been no accidents lately and there is no dwelling on hard luck stories in his conversation.

Mr. Z. enjoys a good social relationship with customers to the liquor store. He talks easily and familiarly with them and they ask for him if Mr. L. happens to be there.

Mr. Z. was very upset when his mistake led to the closing of the store for two weeks. He was depressed once more during that period but recovered soon after the store re-opened.

He boasts about his influence in managing the establishment although Mr. L. does not allow him to make major decisions. He seems to be happy with the position and is no longer anxious about his ability to provide for his family.

father-in-law's advice. Out-
wardly he does not seem per-
turbed by the amount of authority his wife has assumed in
the marriage. He has exhibited
no open resentment about his
wife's close relationship to her
father.

He seems to feel he was
born to bad luck and gets pleasure in recounting examples of it.
He is anxious about his selling
job. Presently he is trying hard
to win a sales contest. There is
some animosity with a distfict
manager who was once his wife's
boy friend. He gets advice from
his wife on how to handle this
man. He also takes her advice
on how to approach other management individuals and how to re-
cruit junior salesmen.

(2) Mrs. Z. is about thirty
pounds overweight and pays little
attention to her appearance. Having few clothes, she spends the
day in old slacks or shorts. Her
speech is rapid and can change
quickly from interest to anger or
animosity. She admits that she
tends to "fly off the handle"
easily and does not mince words.
Her interests center around the
neighborhood and her husband's
job. She would like to be active

He has just joined The
Lions Club and has been nomi-
nated to a Vice Presidency.
This has given him a great
deal of pleasure.

He has to date shown no
animosity to his father-in-law
although he is working directly
under him.

(2) Mrs. Z. has now lost
weight and cut her hair, although she does not frequent
beauty parlors but fixes it at
home. With a better income
she has augmented her wardrobe, although she still wears
slacks for her daily work.

Unlike her husband, she
still indulges in hard luck
stories, recounting the latest
illness of the children or the
latest difficulty at work or

in B'nai B'rith Women, if
she could afford a sitter so
she could attend afternoon
meetings.

Mrs. Z. is usually well
liked. Although decisive,
she has a friendly manner.
Quick to draw others out,
she is equally quick in making up her mind and giving
instructions. She shows little external love in caring
for the children.

She believes that the
family has more than its
share of bad luck, and like
her husband, wallows in
descriptions of misfortune.
She enters into discussions
with relatives, who believe
she is of above average intelligence. She is usually
preoccupied with problems
related to money, insurance,
illness, or her husband's
job.

Mrs. Z. also has fits
of depression and exhibits
great lassitude at times.
Whole days will elapse when
she will sit by a card table
putting puzzles together.
She pulls herself together
enough to direct the children,
do necessary chores, make

school.

She now hires a sitter so
that she can play mah jongg,
thus freeing her mother, and
also so she can attend B'nai
B'rith Women's meetings,
where she has been elected
corresponding secretary.

The days of depression
seem to have gone. She now
exhibits much energy in keeping the house orderely, and
she now has new furniture in
which she takes great pride.

She is attempting to spend
less time with her father.
They have limited visits to
one a week. Her attitude
toward her mother remains
unchanged.

meals and shop. The house, however, is not tidy and her mother often comes in to clean up.

As a neighbor she is constantly involved in swapping favors and spends a good deal of her time talking with neighbors.

She is not happy with her passive husband and looks forward to the companionship of her father. Although she helps drive her mother to required appointments, the older woman's disabilities and tendency to become wordy annoy her, and she finds it most trying to bear her. She will often dismiss her mother in much the same way her father has often done, saying, "Oh, her." or, "You know what she's like."

(3) Jonathan, 9, is tall and husky for his age, dark skinned and curly haired, He cannot sit still long, is very interested in sports. He likes saving money and has begun a bank account. Although he appears to be of average intelligence, and this is borne out by psychological testing, he is slow in learn-

(3) Jonathan has become quieter in school and has made progress in his work since his ear operation. Although he still does not read at grade level, he is no longer required to join a special reading group from a lower grade. His teacher also believes he has displayed less belligerent behavior on the playground.

ing to read and avoids books. School is painful and he has many fights with children, both on the playground and in the classroom. When at home he is always outside, riding his bike and roaming the neighborhood. Other children describe him as belligerent and difficult to get along with.

Through the prodding of his grandmother, a hearing test was arranged for him. It was found that he suffered from a large loss of hearing in one ear. At this writing, they are preparing to hospitalize him for repair.

His problems extend from the peer group into the home. He has been found lighting matches in closets. His mother is attempting to handle this by allowing him to light matches under her supervision.

The match lighting incidents have disappeared.

(4) <u>Danial</u> is 7, blond and short for his age. Perhaps this is why the grandparents still consider him the baby. He is less active than his brother, has a longer span of attention, is learning at school at a normal rate. He gets along well with neighborhood children and is

(4) [Danial] No change.

often invited to parties, swimming pools, etc. He idolizes
his brother and, whenever possible, follows after him in play.

C. CARE AND TRAINING OF CHILDREN

1. Physical Care

Children are well nourished,
clean, adequately clothed.
Jonathan is receiving injections
for an allergy. They use a
doctor whenever there are signs
of illness. Jonathan will soon
be hospitalized for repair of
his ear.

C. 2. Training Methods and Control

There is little overt lov-
ing in this family and praise
is seldom used as an incentive.
The father remains aloof; the
mother often exhibits annoyance.
The children roam the neighborhood with little supervision.

With few rules regulat-
ing their behavior, the boys--
especially Jonathan--seem to
be uncertain about what is expected of them. They are often
in trouble, fighting with others
on the block. For control, the
mother or father will grab a
child and administer a few hard
slaps. There is little carry-over
in setting down rules of behavior,

1. Physical Care

No change.

C. 2. Training Methods and Control

Mrs. Z. is attempting to
use praise more often with the
children, and encouraged by
the social worker, she has
given Jonathan more attention
by helping him with homework
and extending some super-
vision to his play activity.

however. The parents do not
supervise play behavior or
playmates. The boys are never
sure when they will be punished
or what behavior is acceptable.

Mrs. Z. is concerned
about Jonathan's episodes with
fire. Instead of physically
punishing him, she is encouraging him to light matches while
she watches, and she has ex-
plained to him why such behavior
is dangerous.

The parents, upset about
Jonathan's school behavior,
have tried to impress upon
him the importance of listen-
ing to the teacher and being
friendly with schoolmates.
But this plus teacher conferences
have so far made no difference
in the situation.

D.   SOCIAL ACTIVITIES

1.   Informal Associations
The Z.'s meet with the
L.'s, Mrs. Z.'s family, with
the great-grandmother, with
sisters, etc., at least once a
week. They drive down to see
Mr. Z.'s parents at Christmas
and Easter. Holidays are spent
with the extended family. Mrs. Z.
is friendly with her neighbors and
had a neighborhood New Year's
Eve party with six couples.

1.   Informal Associations
Mrs. Z. is attempting to
cut down on her contacts with
family of origin. She has had
peers to dinner and is planning
a party for her sewing club.
The rest is unchanged.

While they always think
of themselves as members of
the neighborhood, they do not
belong to a neighborhood organization. They used the
branch of the Public Library
this year. They discussed
recent city changes in traffic
patterns and store locations
with their sister on her recent
trip home. They actively follow the exploits of their community's high school football
and basketball teams. However,
they take little interest in political contests and do not discuss the social problems of
their community.

The children's standards
of behavior are haphazard,
inconsistent. They have been
taught, however, that there
are certain ways of acting
when they visit their grand-
mothers and they adhere to
these limits.

Free time is spent watch-
ing television, talking with
relatives or neighbors, seeing
a baseball game. Last year
Mr. Z. worked in his basement in the evenings, finishing it off.

D. 2. <u>Formal Associations</u>
   The Z.'s bowl once a

D. 2. <u>Formal Associations</u>
   The Z.'s no longer

month with the company.
Mrs. Z. occasionally attends
a B'nai B'rith Women's meeting. The oldest boy plays in
Little League and the two boys
use the summer playground program.

The Z.'s are not members
of a synagogue or the Jewish
Center because they cannot afford the fees. Jonathan attends
a Temple Hebrew school three
times a week to learn Jewish
History and the Hebrew lang-
uage. The maternal grand-
parents, who are members of
this temple, pay his tuition.

E.   ECONOMIC PRACTICES

  1. Source(s) and Amount
      of Income

Mr. Z., employed by a
national cookware firm, earns
approximately $7,500 a year
with commissions. Neither
life insurance nor health insurance is provided by the
firm. Mr. Z. carries his
GI insurance and has a private health insurance policy
with a high premium. Mrs. Z.
finds it difficult to live within
the income since it fluctuates
from week to week. She food
shops carefully and seldom
buys herself clothing. Much
of the boys' clothing is

regularly bowl. Mrs. Z. attends B'nai B'rith Women and
is an officer. Her husband
attends The Lions, and also
is an officer. Besides Little
League, the two boys now
take swimming lessons at
the Jewish Center, an institution close to their home.

They are now members
of a synagogue. Jonathan
continues to get lessons at
the Hebrew school.

  1. Source(s) and Amount
      of Family Income

Mr. Z. is now employed
by his father-in-law at a liquor
store in an outlying suburb,
earning $13,000 a year. He
still carries his former life
insurance and health policies.

Mrs. Z. has bought her-
self a number of new outfits
and a new coat. Mr. Z. has
supplemented his sport wardrobe. Mrs. Z. has bought
new furniture for the living-
dining room area. They are
now members of the Jewish
Center and they went on a vacation trip this summer.

handed down from Mrs. Z.'s sisters' sons. Her father buys the boys their heavy outerwear each winter. Mr. Z. will buy a suit on sale when necessary.

Mrs. Z. bought inexpensive carpeting for their small home, and--although she is unhappy about its appearance and wear--they are making installment payments on it and also on a second car which they recently acquired. Their living room sofa, bedroom set, boys' beds are all contributions from the extended family. They continue to eat on a card table and chairs bought in their first year of marriage.

Mrs. Z. is very bitter because they have never taken a vacation. When Mr. Z. takes a few days off during the year they drive down to see his parents. She is very envious of her sisters and other family members who manage annual trips. She is also envious of other members who maintain Center memberships and send children to camp. Although the family cannot be considered deprived--food, shelter, and a minimum of

Mrs. Z. continues to be a careful shopper and the pattern of dressing the boys in hand-me-downs continues.

clothing is provided--it is
straining to maintain itself
on the present income level.

E. 2. Job Situation

Mr. Z. is a salesman
for a cookware firm which is
decentralized, though national,
and which expects him to spend
some of his time without re-
muneration enlisting and training new applicants. He must
buy his samples and the free
wares he leaves at each door
from the company and is required to eat lunch at a
restaurant twice a week with
other area salesmen--all
these expenses substantially
reduce his take-home pay.

He seems to get along
well with co-workers, but his
district manager is an old
beau of his wife's and he
feels insecure and inferior
working under him. He is
essentially dissatisfied with
the job, although he is afraid
that this feeling testifies to
his inadequacies. From time
to time he tries to apply for
other jobs, but he does so
in a half-hearted manner and
finds--or says he finds--it
very difficult to take the time
off for interviews.

E. 2. Job Situation

Mr. Z., now working for
his father-in-law, has a schedule of hours, responsibilities,
and pay which makes him hap-
pier. In the beginning he
began to make decisions about
buying and selling which his
father-in-law later counter-
manded. He now acts strictly
as a clerk, and although he
has grumbled to his wife about
this, he has accepted it more
or less gracefully.

He was very morose after
the run-in with the police when
the liquor license was temporarily revoked. His father-in-
law rebuked him very sharply,
and there was a recurrence of
debilitating depression. When
the store reopened this disappeared. He brags to out-
siders that he is the boss,
but his wife, who knows better,
remains quietly loyal.

There are continuing crises
which try the father-in-law's
patience and short temper.
But until now the situation has
remained satisfactory.

He has been working for this firm six years and his wife is accustomed to his hours. She helps him a great deal keeping accounts, filling orders, answering the telephone about training new salesmen, but she is often angry about giving so much extra time. Still she prefers the security of this position to the insecurity they experienced when he was trying to sell insurance. The children, largely unaffected by their father's job, are perhaps inconvenienced at certain times when the filling of orders makes them stay out of the recreation room.

E. 3. Use of Money

Mr. Z. seems to be very happy with the present arrangement concerning the management of his salary. His wife not only pays bills and doles out allowances but also makes the decisions about when to buy what. She consults her father on matters of insurance and interest and used his advice in buying their home. They have no savings. Mr. Z. has GI insurance and a private medical insurance policy. Two items which Mrs. Z. bought upon purchasing their home

E. 3. Use of Money

Mrs. Z. continues to make decisions about the allocation of money. Under Mr. L's prodding, they have started a small savings account. Mrs. Z. bought new furniture for their home. They have finished paying for the garage and carpeting, and their debts now include payments on the car and on the new furniture. Mrs. Z. now admits that she enjoys making decisions about spending money.

were considered extravagant
by her parents--custom made
drapes and wall-to-wall carpeting. Her husband, however,
concurred with her decision.
The second car might also be
termed an extravagance, but
both the Z.'s insist that she
needs transportation during the
day while he needs the car for
work. Thus their debts now
include payments for the carpeting and the new car. They also
owe money on a garage. The
builder for the garage they con-
tracted filed bankruptcy halfway
through construction and then
disappeared. They could not
recover the money which they
had prepaid and, because of a
clause in the contract, they also
found themselves liable to the
bank for the entire amount. Thus,
they were required by law to pay
twice for an uncompleted structure.
Although they consulted Mr. L.'s
lawyer, they found they had no
choice but to make payments to
the bank (see also E. 1.).

F.   HOME AND HOUSEHOLD
      PRACTICES

1. Physical Facilities

The Z.'s own their home, a
three-bedroom ranch in a development of ninety homes which was
built about six years ago. The

1. Physical Facilities

The Z.'s live in the same
home. The recreation room is
now habitable but the children
still use the living room for

rooms are small but the kitchen is large enough for the
family to take their meals
there.   Each boy has a room
of his own.   There is one small
bathroom which seems sufficient
for the size and age of the family.   The basement has been
converted into a recreation
room, but a good part of it
is filled with boxes of materials
for orders.   The Z.'s have
painted the house once since they
moved in.   The grounds are
kept in relatively good condition,
and a half-finished garage is in
the deep backyard which also has
a swing set (a present from a
sister) and old lawn furniture.

The neighborhood is resi-
dential, an outlying section of a
medium sized New Jersey community.   The homes are all the
same age and type.   There is
little traffic on the street.
Children play on the lawns and
in the backyards; the school and
Jewish Center are just three and
four blocks away.

The Z.'s own a large re-
frigerator, washer, and dryer,
all bought when they were first
married.   The living room sofa
was given them by Mrs. L.; they
have a television set and card-

play.   The garage is still half
finished.

Old dilapidated furnishings
have been replaced.   There is
new furniture in the living room--
sofa, chairs, tables--and a
dinette set in the kitchen.

table upon which they eat. Their
bedroom set was sent by Mr. Z. 's
parents and the boys' beds and
chests came from miscellaneous
relatives.

F. 2. Housekeeping Standards

Inside, the home is rather
neglected. The children play in
the living room rather than the
basement, and the litter is seldom picked up. Garbage sits
in paper bags in the kitchen.
The counterspace is limited
in the kitchen and always over-
flowing with food, notes, etc.
The beds are left unmade and
dust is not vacuumed. There is
little attempt to keep the home
attractive, although the taste-
ful color scheme, carpeting,
and drapes testify to the fact
that at one time this must have
been important to Mrs. Z.

Household chores are car-
ried out by Mrs. Z. The
cleaning and straightening, when
done, are her responsibilities,
as are the dishes, the cooking,
and laundry. The boys are supposed to make their own beds in
the morning but this is often
forgotten or done poorly. Mr. Z.
empties the garbage at night and
is supposed to clean up in the
recreation room every week

F. 2. Housekeeping Standards

Chores are still appor-
tioned in the same way. The
inside of the house is kept
cleaner. The garbage is no
longer standing in the kitchen.
Mrs. Z. attempts to keep the
living room cleaner, but the
boys' rooms are still in dis-
array.

Mrs. Z. continues to
shop carefully, using food ads
when possible. Meals are the
same, but more expensive
cuts of meat occasionally appear.

Clothing is apportioned
similarly, with the exception
of Mrs. Z. 's wardrobe. She
has bought both sport and dress
clothing, with a sister as an
adviser. Her buying has remained in the moderate price
range, although she has been
encouraged to spend more by
her wealthier sister. Mr. Z.
has bought slacks and sport
shirts to wear in the liquor
store.

The Z. 's bought new

after orders are filled, but these tasks are most often neglected.

Meals are served on a regular schedule, with the most substantial meal in the evening when all are home. Mrs. Z. knows a great deal about nutrition, buys wisely, and serves a variety of dishes, many of them never made in her own child-hood home. There is a great deal of snacking, and consequently the boys eat little at their regular meals. Mrs. Z. seldom prohibits their foraging for food between meals since she herself is a nibbler. Both she and her husband enjoy eating and cooking, and he often helps cook on weekends. Some of the new dishes are from his repertoire. Whenever possible he barbecues on Sunday.

The major portion of their weekly income goes for food. Mrs. Z. shops for groceries at a discount store quite a distance from their home where slightly damaged canned goods or mangled chickens can be gotten for less. They try to use hand-me-downs for the children but buy all shoes at reputable shoe stores.

furniture for the living room, dining room, and kitchen. Mrs. Z. would like to replace the draperies and carpeting too, but wistfully adds she knows it cannot be done at this time.

They took their first vacation this summer, renting a camper and traveling to state parks.

Outer clothing is donated by
Mr. L. Mr. Z. buys a suit
on sale every three or four
years. Mrs. Z. buys little
clothing. They recently acquired a second car, used.
No furniture purchases have
been made in the past six
years. Materials for the
finishing of the basement
were bought last year and
they are making payments
on the ill-fated garage. They
take no trips or vacations,
although they drive down to
see Mr. Z.'s parents once a
year. They do not often hire
sitters. They have an individual health insurance plan and
pay for drugs and doctor's
visits at each health emer-
gency.

G.   HEALTH CONDITIONS AND
     PRACTICES

1.   Health Conditions

Mr. Z. has injuries from
two accidents which occurred during the past year: in the first
instance he fell into a hole
near a new building while
making his selling rounds,
and in the second, he was
struck from behind by another
vehicle while waiting to make
a turn in his car. His arm,

1.   Health Conditions

Mr. Z.'s back no longer
bothers him although he sometimes suffers pain when moving
heavy cases in the liquor store.

Mrs. Z. is in good health;
she still suffers colds.

Jonathan was operated on
and the operation was termed
successful. He is doing better work in school.

shoulder, and back give him pain. He has been going to a private doctor for almost a year and wears a back brace. Although the car claim was settled, the other claim he filed for negligence is still outstanding, since neither the contractor nor the house owner wishes to accept responsibility. The soreness of his back and arm make it difficult for him to carry his sample case.

Mrs. Z. is in good physical condition. Whenever the children have colds, however, she is prone to catch them, remaining ill for three or more weeks during which time she finds it impossible to carry on with household tasks.

Jonathan has a hearing defect which has just been detected. Other than that, he seems normal. Testing in school and at agency has revealed no learning disability despite his school difficulties.

Danial wears glasses for a slight cross-eyed condition. Otherwise healthy.

G. 2. Health Practices

The family obtains medical care from private physicians whenever necessary. They follow

G. 2. Health Practices

No change.

the medical advice given them and buy prescribed medications.

They follow middle-class hygiene practices as far as food preparation, dishwashing, personal cleanliness are concerned.

They do not have regular dental checkups (Mrs. Z. cannot justify the expense) but use a dentist when necessary. Mrs. Z. and Danial had dental work this year. Neither adults nor children make a practice of regularly brushing their teeth.

H.   RELATIONSHIP TO SOCIAL WORKER

1.   Attitude toward Worker

Mrs. Z. made inquiries, contacted the agency on her own. She is very cooperative, sincerely wishes to accurately describe the home situation and gain help from worker. After two visits, though, she expressed some doubt about the worker's ability to help. Mr. Z. insisted they had no problems and refused to come to either interview. Mrs. Z. is seen twice a month, while Jonathan is seeing a psychologist and is undergoing psychometric testing.

1.   Attitude toward Worker

Mrs. Z., who attends monthly sessions, is grateful to the worker for the changes which have been made in her relationship and for her better understanding of herself and the family situation. However, she expresses the feeling that more of the improvements in family life were due to a change in employment than to social work treatment. Mr. Z. attends sessions, is no longer as defensive and exhibits some gratitude to worker. Jonathan has also been seen jointly with his parents at irregular intervals.

H. 2. Use of Worker

Mrs. Z. is using the worker both to vent her feelings about her husband and to gain advice in the inter-personal areas of family life. She would like to effect change in her relationship with Mr. Z. and thus create a less tense home atmosphere. Some of the second session was devoted to describing her feelings about her children and parents. The worker is encouraging her to find new ways of dealing with her older son. Mr. Z. has been invited to come but has found himself "too busy" to attend the sessions.

I. USE OF COMMUNITY RESOURCES

1. School

Both parents want their children to be successful in school. They have expressed a desire to have them go through college, although at the moment they do not know how they could manage it financially. They insist the children attend regularly, be on time, do homework. Mrs. Z. attends when the children are in special programs. She has

H. 2. Use of Worker

Mrs. Z. no longer uses the worker to vent feelings, but rather as a resource to give advice and to help achieve understanding. Mr. Z. uses the worker as adviser but not as a help toward understanding underlying psychological mechanisms.

1. School

Jonathan is reading better since his ear operation and is less aggressive. He is continuing in Hebrew School because of his improved functioning and is generally on a par with the others in his class. Mrs. Z. has become an active member of the elementary school P. T. A. and the parent's association of the Hebrew School.

had conferences with Jonathan's teachers during which
his reading difficulties and
aggression have been discussed.
She contacted the school nurse
about Jonathan's hearing difficulties before a private physician was consulted. The
nurse gave him preliminary
testing and then suggested
they see a physician.

Jonathan uses any excuse
to stay away from school. He
does not do the extra homework which was given him to
improve his reading. In
fact, attempts to make him
do the work at home created
so much trouble (crying, anger)
that Mrs. Z. has given up trying to work with him after
school.

He also attends Hebrew
classes two days a week after
school and each Sunday morning. They have received reports of trouble from his teacher also and are thinking of letting him drop these classes altogether since his difficulties
seem to increase on those
days when he is expected to
sit still for long periods of
time.

Danial, on the other hand,

has proved cooperative and
successful in school. He has
not yet started Hebrew
School.

I. 2.   Church

The family is not a mem-
ber of a congregation because
they cannot afford the membership fee. They attend High
Holy Day services at the
parents' synagogue (tickets
for these services are sold
separately), sharing three
seats among the four of
them. A few times a year
on special holidays they attend
services at the L.'s synagogue,
bringing the boys with them for
purposes of introducing the boys
to the holiday and the ritual.
As noted, Jonathan attends a
Hebrew School affiliated with
the grandparents' synagogue.
The Z.'s feel it is important
to transmit culture and religion
to their children and feel
strongly about attendance at
such a school.

I. 3.   Health Resources

The Z.'s use private
doctors and dentists, patron-
ize private pharmacies. The
use of the school nurse for
hearing tests is unusual for

I. 2.   Church

The family has joined the
parents' synagogue and pays
$150 dues a year. They at-
tend services on an average
of ten times a year. Mrs. Z.
has become an active member
of the Sisterhood.

I. 3.   Health Resources

No change.

they usually use private
facilities.

I. 4.   Social Agencies

Mrs. Z. cooperates with
the local Family Service Agency and believes they will help
her marriage.   She feels they
helped her in the past and will
do so in the present.   Mr. Z.
is resentful, defensive, ashamed
to be connected with the agency.

They do not make use of
other agencies.

I. 5.   Recreational Agencies

The Z.'s use the summer
playground program and library
for their children.   Jonathan
plays in Little League.   They
do not use Boy Scout or similar programs.

The Z.'s use town parks,
swimming lakes and state
shore facilities.   They cannot
afford the Jewish Center facilities or private pools.   They
have never tried the "Y" which
is situated a long distance
from their house.

I. 4.   Social Agencies

Mr. Z. exhibits less de-
fensive and shamed behavior
but has mentioned that they
can now terminate agency
help since they seem to be
doing better.

I. 5.   Recreational Agencies

They now use the Jewish
Center facilities as paying
members.   Otherwise no
change.

On the following pages ratings on the social functioning of the
Z. family, separated as to beginning and after situations, are presented.   The rating was done by three independent individuals, all
of whom had previous experience in this type of coding.   On all
main categories and all sub-categories but one, health conditions,
the three raters either agreed on scores (50. 7%) or two agreed

while the third checked the adjacent position (49. 3%).   (There was
a difference of opinion about the seriousness of the health problems
in the beginning situation; one rater coded them as marginal while
the other two evaluated them as near adequate.)   Where coders
disagreed as described above, the scores which are shown represent the majority view, that is, the concurrence of two coders.
On health conditions, a near adequate rating was agreed upon at a
conference of the three.   Score sheets for beginning and after situations and for movement, with a graphic movement Profile as well,
follow the discussion of the ratings.

RATIONALE FOR SCORE ASSIGNED

Category	Beg.	After

Sub-Category:

Marital Relationship	5	Conflict for this couple revolves around unfulfilled aspirations and needs--wealth and social position. The hus- band is unable to measure up to expectations. A rating of 4 would be too low, since both spouses express concern for the relationship and a need to maintain the partnership, even though the wife does not respect the husband's position in the family. Routineness seems more the pattern than pleasure in the relationship. Lack of communi- cation and inability to talk through their feelings pervade the situation. Hence a rating of 5--above marginal rather than 6--near adequate.

Sub-Category:	Beg.	After

Marital Relationship (continued) — After: 6

Despite some continued reticense about open discussion, there is considerably more pleasure derived from this marriage than earlier. Each partner can perform his tasks more confidently, though Mr. Z. had some problems in this new job.

Sub-Category:

Parent-Child Relationship — Beg: 5

Since consistency of treatment and impartiality are not strong points in this family, the rating hovers around marginal. The mother reacts erratically and the father is indifferent until he explodes. The partiality shown to the younger child is clearly not desirable.

After: 6

Many of the conditions remain the same--inability to show affection, indifference, erratic and inconsistent discipline. But the conscious effort to relate, to treat the children more equally, and the awareness of the need to create a new climate enables us to rate this household near adequate.

Sub-Category:

Sibling Relationship — Beg: 7

Determining how much "sibling rivalry" is acceptable within a family is difficult, and while we do not wish to perpetuate the "boys will be

Sub-Category:	Beg.	After

Sibling
Relationship
(continued)

boys" theory, it is evident that the younger child admires his brother and that the older, though somewhat jealous, cares for his little brother. We cannot expect all possessions to be shared or all of their time to be spent together.

There is nothing here to suggest an atypical problem or severe conflict, and since there are many positives, we consider this 7--adequate.

7   The basic attitudes and behavior remain the same.

Sub-Category:		

Family   6
Solidarity

Clearly, the near marginal 5 or less is not applicable because the Z.'s are a solidary family, but some soul searching is required to make the distinction between 6 and 7. This family obviously operates as a cohesive unit--they eat together, spend leisure time together; certainly their goals are consistent with community standards. Even the wife's dependence upon her own father, while in some circumstances undesirable, does not diminish the rating, since the husband does not seem to resent it.

Sub-Category:	Beg.	After

Family Solidarity (continued)

Here, the missing link is "satisfaction," "warmth and affection" derived from the togetherness, preventing an outright 7.

7

While much of the behavior is the same, the whole atmosphere in the family is marked by greater satisfaction. Individuals are making conscious efforts to improve the emotional feeling.

Main Category

FAMILY RELA-TIONSHIP AND UNITY   5

Greatest weight is placed on the relationship involving Mr. and Mrs. Z., which dominates the family picture. This rating also reflects the general shortcomings in the parent-child relationships.

6

An overall rating of 6 indicates a near adequate marital relationship in the after situation and a parent-child relationship--also rated 6--that is guided by some awareness of problems and efforts to overcome them.

Sub-Category:

Father   5

Law violations do not enter this picture. Mr. Z. gets along with people, but he often becomes depressed, his self-image is poor (he dwells on

Sub-Category:	Beg.	After

Father
(continued)

hard luck), and he tends to become immobilized under stress.
Regarding various areas of role
performance the rating is below
adequate. He respects his
spouse but is in conflict with
her; he cares for his children
but withdraws from a positive
parental role, over-emphasizing
punishment or keeping aloof.
Not strong as a breadwinner,
he does work and cares about
his performance in this role.
Weighing the relative strengths
and weaknesses, Mr. Z. falls
most appropriately into 5.

6

Mr. Z.'s new job has re-
inforced some character posi-
tives--i. e. , the ability to get
along with people. The improvement in earning capacity has
given him additional confidence,
warranting a higher rating.

Sub-Category:

Mother   5

Mrs. Z.'s poor appearance
and her complaining attest to
her poor self-image. Obviously
unhappy with her social position
and the lack of extra income,
she is still functioning above
the marginal (4) level since
her behavior does not represent
a potential threat to the welfare

Sub-Category:	Beg.	After

Mother
(continued)

of the family.   There are disagreements and conflicts and
hostility toward Mr. Z. , but
she, nonetheless, helps him
with his work, responds to
need.

Display of affection is
limited and favoritism toward
one child might indicate a marginal rating, yet physical care
is adequate and her interest and
concern are not questioned.

She is well liked, gregar-
ious, but dissatisfied with her
limited participation in outside
groups.   Generally, satisfaction
in the homemaking role is so
limited that a rating of 5 is indicated.

7

There is so much change
in Mrs. Z. 's appearance (weight-
loss, additional clothing), role
performance (club participation,
housekeeping), mental state
(fewer depressions, added
energy), that the jump to 7
is warranted.

Sub-Category:

Children   5

Jonathan, the older child,
seems to fit the marginal description: acting-out behavior,
receiving treatment for possible
emotional disorder, school performance below capacity,

Sub-Category:	Beg.	After

Children
(continued)

physical handicap necessitating treatment, less than adequate relationship with parents, and poor attitudes toward school. Although he "lights matches" the behavior is not clearly delinquent, but by the criteria applied here it does not exceed the marginal level.

Danial, however, so fits into the adequate area that we set a 5 for the combined rating.

6   Jonathan has made considerable progress--he has been treated for his hearing problem, he is less belligerent, more conforming to norms. With Danial's functioning remaining at the adequate level, we decide on a combined rating of 6 rather than 7, for Jonathan continues to have problems at school.

Main Category

INDIVIDUAL   5   This is the mean and modal
BEHAVIOR   rating for all family members.

6   This rating represents the predominate rating of Individual Behavior and Adjustment in the after situation.

Sub-Category:

Physical Care   7   Everything herein fits the adequate description.

7   Same as before.

Sub-Category:	Beg.	After

Training   5
Methods and
Emotional
Care

The parents being incon-
sistent, clearly showing favoritism to the younger child, not
defining limits of acceptable
behavior would generally fit
into the marginal description.

But because there is positive feeling, there is concern
for the children, and there is
no deviancy from community
norms, we consider 4 too low
and 5 more appropriate.

                 6

Attempts are being made by
the parents to reinforce good behavior, give praise, and to show
attention to Jonathan, thereby
diminishing the "favoritism"
accusation.

Main Category

CARE AND   5
TRAINING OF
CHILDREN

Clearly training methods
carry most weight in giving a
category score.

                 6

Near adequate functioning
is evident as parents make con-
certed effort to remedy deficien-
cies in child rearing.

Sub-Category:

Informal   7
Associations

Consistent with "adequate"
description. Relationships with
family and friends are good;
both Mr. and Mrs. Z. are
friendly and well-liked; and
there is general agreement on

Sub-Category:	Beg.	After

| Informal Associations (continued) | | | leisure time activities between the two. |
| | | 7 | Same as before. |

Sub-Category:

| Formal Associations | 6 | | Although there is a positive attitude toward organizations to which they belong, there is frustration over their inability to join the Jewish Center, suggesting that a 6 rather than a 7 rating is most appropriate. |
| | | 7 | The family is now in a position to make good use of formal organizations. |

Main Category

| SOCIAL ACTIVITIES | 7 | | Social activities are preponderately adequate. |
| | | 7 | No change from the before situation. |

Sub-Category:

| Source and Amount of Income | 5 | | Although family is dissatisfied with marginal, somewhat irregular income, Mr. Z. is working regularly and needs are met, even if there are no extras. |
| | | 7 | There is a substantial improvement in this situation. Income has increased, allowing for some extras, and the family enjoys more security. |

Sub-Category:

| Job Situation | 5 | | Mr. Z. 's work pattern is |

Sub-Category:	Beg.	After	

Job Situation
(continued)

steady although it is apparent he is dissatisfied with the job and frustrated over his inability to get a better position.

7   Mr. Z. is obviously more suited to his new role and pleased with the situation.

Sub-Category:

Use of Money   6   Despite some bad debts, management of money and payment of the debts is planned. The major dissension is in the wife's resentment of her role as manager.

7   Now that Mrs. Z. has not only adjusted to but acknowledged her liking for the responsibility of money manager, the rating has risen to 7.

Main Category:

ECONOMIC   5   The prevailing feeling of
PRACTICES dissatisfaction in each area puts the overall rating at 5, or above marginal.

7   An overall after rating of 7 is identical with each subcategory rating and reflects the basically positive outlook in this area.

Sub-Category:

Physical   6   The neighborhood in which
Facilities the Z.'s live is pleasant, and though the home is small, each

Sub-Category:	Beg.	After

Physical
Facilities
(continued)

child has his own room. The
main qualifying factors are the
"takeover" of the basement by
the merchandise samples, an
arrangement limiting the boys'
play area and contributing to
the dissatisfaction of Mrs. Z.

7

With the removal of the
samples the family can better
utilize the basement space.

Sub-Category:

Housekeeping 6
Standards

Although the home may be
in some disorder, it is far from
hazardous to the welfare of the
children. Meals are adequate
and certainly hygiene standards
are satisfactory.

7

Improvement in housekeeping
standards is another indication of
positive changes this family has
been experiencing.

Main Category:

HOUSEHOLD 6
PRACTICES

The main category rating of
6 corresponds to the sub-category
ratings.

7

Rating is the same as the
sub-category ratings.

Sub-Category:

Health 6
Conditions

Back problems and some
weaknesses in carrying sample
cases are noted, but they do
not interfere seriously with
Mr. Z.'s ability to earn a

Sub-Category:	Beg.	After

Health Conditions (continued)

living. Nor can Mrs. Z.'s frequent colds be said to limit her functioning.

Jonathan's hearing loss is being investigated, although its effect upon his poor school performance is conjectural.

7   No major health problems are noted in the after situation.

Sub-Category:

Health Practices   7

Both general hygiene and attention to health are adequate, as is the Z.'s pursuit of proper medical resources.

7   The same high standards prevail.

Main Category:

HEALTH CONDITIONS AND PRACTICES   6

This rating takes into account the health problems that exist at this time.

7   Overall functioning is adequate with regard to health situation and practices.

Sub-Category:

Attitude toward Worker   6

Mr. Z.'s resistance to treatment is overshadowed by the response of the rest of the family.

7   With the father's reluctance overcome, the family reveals a basically favorable attitude toward professional services.

Sub-Category:	Beg.	After

| Use of Worker | 6 | | Mr. Z.'s resistance does not permit optimum use of the worker. |
| | | 7 | Positive use of the worker by both parents justifies this rating. |

Main Category

| RELATIONSHIP TO WORKER | 6 | | The before rating of the main category is in line with the sub-category ratings. |
| | | 7 | The overall after rating is the same as the sub-category ratings. |

Sub-Category:

| Schools | 6 | | Jonathan's problems in school make this a near adequate rather than adequate rating. |
| | | 7 | With improvement in Jonathan's school behavior, the family's use of resources may be rated 7. |

Sub-Category:

| Church | N.A. | | Occasional attendance but nonmembership dictates a "not applicable" rating. |
| | | 7 | Membership in the synagogue and attendance at services makes this a 7 rating. |

Sub-Category:

| Health Resources | 7 | | This family utilizes available medical resources. |

Sub-Category:	Beg.	After	
		7	No change.
Sub-Category:			
Social Agencies	6		Some problems in the rela-tionship to the Family Service Agency makes this only a near adequate rating.
		7	Social agencies are well utilized in the after situation.
Sub-Category:			
Recreation Agencies	7		This family makes exten-sive and good use of recreational resources and facilities.
		7	Same as in the before situa-tion.
Main Category:			
USE OF COMMUNITY RESOURCES	7		The positive attitude toward and the reasonably good use of most of the community's resour-ces justifies an overall rating of 7 or adequate, despite the 6 ratings in two sub-categories.
		7	The positive approach to the available community re-sources is maintained.

PROFILE OF MOVEMENT

ON Z FAMILY

MAIN CATEGORIES	Minus 3	Minus 2	Minus 1	No Change	Plus 1	Plus 2	Plus 3	Plus 4
Family Relationships								
Individual Behavior								
Care and Training of Children								
Social Activities								
Economic Practices								
Home and Household Practices								
Health Conditions								
Relationship to Worker								
Use of Community Resources								

Joint Ratings

FINAL SCORES
PROFILE OF FAMILY FUNCTIONING

Family:___Z___ Case No.:_____ Scorer(s):___Three Independent Raters___

1st Profile ___X___
2nd   "   _____
3rd   "   _____
4th   "   _____
5th   "   _____
6th   "   _____

	Not Known	Not App.	Category Score	Sub-Category Score
FAMILY RELATIONSHIPS			5	
Marital Relationship				5
Parent-Child Relationship				5
Sibling Relationship				7
Family Solidarity				6
Relationship with other Household Members		X		
INDIVIDUAL BEHAVIOR			5	
Father				5
Mother				5
Older Children (10 & up)		X		
Younger Children (1-9)				5
CARE AND TRAINING OF CHILDREN			5	
Physical Care				7
Training Methods				5
SOCIAL ACTIVITIES			7	
Informal Associations				7
Formal Associations				6
ECONOMIC PRACTICES			5	
Source of Income				5
Job Situation				5
Use of Money				6

	Not Known	Not App.	Category Score	Sub-Category Score
HOME AND HOUSEHOLD PRACTICES			6	
Physical Facilities				6
Housekeeping Standards				6
HEALTH CONDITIONS & PRACTICES			6	
Health Conditions				6
Health Practices				7
RELATIONSHIP TO WORKER			6	
Attitude Toward Worker				6
Use of Worker				6
USE OF COMMUNITY RE- SOURCES			7	
School				6
Church		X		
Health Resources				7
Social Agencies				6
Recreational Agencies				7

FINAL SCORES
PROFILE OF FAMILY FUNCTIONING

Family:____Z____Case No.:_____Scorer(s):_____ Three Independent Raters

1st Profile_____
2nd   "   ___X___
3rd   "   _____
4th   "   _____
5th   "   _____
6th   "   _____

	Not Known	Not App.	Category Score	Sub-Category Score
FAMILY RELATIONSHIPS			6	
Marital Relationship				6
Parent-Child Relationship				6
Sibling Relationship				7
Family Solidarity				7
Relationship with other Household Members		X		
INDIVIDUAL BEHAVIOR			6	
Father				6
Mother				7
Older Children (10 & up)		X		
Younger Children (1-9)				6
CARE AND TRAINING OF CHILDREN			6	
Physical Care				7
Training Methods				6
SOCIAL ACTIVITIES			7	
Informal Associations				7
Formal Associations				7
ECONOMIC PRACTICES			7	
Source of Income				7
Job Situation				7
Use of Money				7

	Not Known	Not App.	Category Score	Sub-Category Score
HOME AND HOUSEHOLD PRACTICES			7	
Physical Facilities				7
Housekeeping Standards				7
HEALTH CONDITIONS & PRACTICES			7	
Health Problems				7
Health Practices				7
RELATIONSHIP TO WORKER			7	
Attitude Toward Worker				7
Use of Worker				7
USE OF COMMUNITY RE-SOURCES			7	
School				7
Church				7
Health Resources				7
Social Agencies				7
Recreational Agencies				7

FINAL SCORES
PROFILE OF FAMILY FUNCTIONING

Family: ___Z___ Case No.: _____ Scorer(s): ___Three Independent Raters___

Change Profile	Not Known	Not App.	Category Score	Sub-Category Score
FAMILY RELATIONSHIPS			+1	
Marital Relationship				+1
Parent-Child Relation-ship				+1
Sibling Relationship				0
Family Solidarity				0
Relationship with other Household Members		X*		
INDIVIDUAL BEHAVIOR			+1	
Father				+1
Mother				+2
Other Children (10 & up)		X*		
Younger Children (1-9)				+1
CARE AND TRAINING OF CHILDREN			+1	
Physical Care				0
Training Methods				+1
SOCIAL ACTIVITIES			0	
Informal Associations				0
Formal Associations				+1
ECONOMIC PRACTICES			+2	
Source of Income				+2
Job Situation				+2
Use of Money				+1

*No change rating can be assigned when either beginning or after rating or both are missing.

	Not Known	Not App.	Category Score	Sub-Category Score
HOME AND HOUSEHOLD PRACTICES			+1	
Physical Facilities				+1
Housekeeping Facilities				+1
HEALTH CONDITIONS & PRACTICES			+1	
Health Problems				+1
Health Practices				0
RELATIONSHIP TO WORKER			+1	
Attitude Toward Worker				+1
Use of Worker				+1
USE OF COMMUNITY RESOURCES			0	
School				+1
Church		X*		
Health Resources				0
Social Agencies				+1
Recreational Agencies				0

*No change rating can be assigned when either beginning or after rating or both are missing.

IV. 6. Statistical Issues in Data Analysis

As we have stated earlier, the family functioning scale was designed to assess the social functioning of seriously disorganized families.   The score continuum which ranges from 1 to 7, adequate to inadequate, was set up to cover all forms of behavior encountered in family research, with the marginal position of 4 considered the theoretical mid-point around which the functioning of problematic families would cluster.

Early studies with multi-problem families showed that while some areas and sub-categories--particularly those representing expressive behavior--showed a reasonably normal distribution around a mean of 4 or less, other areas were skewed in the direction of better behavior.   Two studies based on samples of lower-class, seriously problematic families showed overall means for nine areas of 3. 85 and 4. 38, respectively. [19] Research with less deprived families shows higher mean scores with more skewing in the direction of adequate functioning. [20]   Also, while samples of multi-problem families yielded score distributions which met requirements for Gutman scalability, [21] the scores of less problematic populations were not scalable.   This variability in score characteristics, reflecting, of course, differences in functioning traits, must be taken into account when analyzing data.   The following guidelines were designed to be of help in this situation.

When scores are reasonably well distributed and not unduly skewed in any area, analysis can take into account all or nearly all the score positions (given a large enough sample) and utilize parametric statistical techniques.   When scores are skewed and/or the distribution has a limited spread, data can be handled most appropriately by combining score positions and employing statistical devices which are nonparametric.

An alternate technique, especially appropriate if the data prove to be nonscalable, is factor analysis.   The goal here is to reduce a large number of items to sets of common factors or

dimensions.   Factor analysis of the Family Functioning Profile
should be based on the most basic units of observation, the 26 sub-
categories rather than the nine main areas, which are likely to
constitute main foci of the analysis. [22]

Another scale refinement which might be contemplated is
multi-variate analysis, a method which offers the opportunity to
develop area weights which can then be used to score the total
social functioning of a family.   It is clear that the contribution
of each area to overall family functioning varies considerably,
depending on such factors as family size, life-cycle stage, social
class, and others.   In our presently used method of analysis, each
area has been given equal weight in the total score, and the area
interrelationships are examined afterwards by means of Gutman
scaling or correlational analysis.   In multi-variate analysis a
weighting system would be developed so that the total family scores
would be based on weighted sub-scores, reflecting the contribution
of each area to overall family functioning within a given universe
of families.

IV. 7.   Reliability and Validity

Ever since the present scale for measuring the social
functioning of families--or an earlier version of it--was developed,
the problems of reliability and validity have received much attention.   Before we examine these issues, a few words of caution to
the researcher.   When reliability tests have had positive results,
they have been interpreted by the researcher as constituting a mandate for the instrument's use.   This writer wishes to stress, however, the importance of continuing reliability tests in future
measurement endeavors, regardless of the positive results which
have been reported in the past.   Test reliability, after all, is a
function of the performance of people and not the quality of the
instrument alone.

The present discussion of efforts aimed at establishing

reliability and validity will be limited to just a few of the more notable attempts, allowing the reader who is interested in specifics to explore the citations in depth.

Reliability

In the original manual on the measurement of family functioning two types of reliability were examined: inter-rater reliability at coding, which tested the consistency with which two or more raters coded the narrative Profile, and the reliability of schedule writing, or the degree to which different people who read the same case material conceptualize and profile the material in the same way. [23] The latter issue is rarely dealt with in the social science literature, because it is generally assumed that a clear conceptual scheme furnishes a built-in reliability.

Carrying out a reliability test of profile writing is, of course, contingent upon having a reliable technique of rating family functioning. Both types of reliability were tested with the aid of three independent raters and Profile writers, and results indicated at least a minimal measure of reliability. [24]

The recommended procedure for reliability testing is to have three independent coders read each case and compare scores. One method of establishing criteria of inter-rater agreement is to count the percentage of ratings where three raters agree on the same scale position, where two raters agree on the same position while one checks an adjacent position, and where each rater checks a different position. If the first two alternatives can be considered acceptable reliability, the proportion of ratings meeting these conditions may be taken as an index of reliability. Tests with data in the Neighborhood Improvement Project showed reliability percentages for rating beginning position and movement to be 87.4% and 97.4%, respectively. [25]

Another aspect of inter-rater reliability was examined in the Chemung County Research Demonstration with Dependent Multi-Problem Families. In this experimental-control study of the effects of casework intervention, two different teams of raters who coded identical Profiles were compared. The principal investigator reported very similar results for the two teams, each of which was affiliated with a different organization. [26]

Validity

Although more difficult to demonstrate than reliability, validity is the ultimate criterion of a measuring instrument's utility. We shall seek to bring evidence of two types of validity for the Family Functioning Scale: Internal validity, or the consistency with which the several items tap the same dimension, [27] or simply hang together; and external validity, or the extent to which test results coincide with other known measures of the same dimension.

The strongest evidence of internal validity was supplied by its ability to meet Gutman scale requirements when an analysis of a sample of 150 lower-class, socially disorganized families was carried out. [28] It was found that Profile scores for a random sample of 555 young, urban families did not meet scalability requirements, but inter-correlations among areas of social functioning were all significant above the . 001 level and ranged from r's of . 578 to . 779 for correlations between area score and total score, and r's from . 378 to . 807 for intercorrelations among eight areas of social functioning. [29] (The area Relationship to the Social Worker was not included because the research population was not receiving services.)

External validity was tested in one instance by independent interviews with husbands and wives (N=40) and a comparison of their responses on 19 items and 6 dimensions of behavior and beliefs in family life. The test was based on the assumption that husband-wife agreement regarding various aspects of family functioning is evidence of that fact that their independent reports correspond to the actual situation and may, therefore, be considered valid. Agreement ratios ranged from . 73 to . 93, with a mean of . 80 and a standard deviation of . 067. [30]

A more rigorous test of external validity was provided by comparing the results of movement measured by the Family Functioning Scale with those obtained by another standardized instrument, the Community Service Scale, also known as the Hunt-Kogan Scale, which measures change due to social service intervention. The occasion for this validity test was the above mentioned Chemung County Study. Results of the measurement of outcome on the two movement scales for both experimental and control groups were very similar. A comparison of ratings for identical cases showed that "in more than 40 percent of the cases the ratings were the same, while in another 40 percent the differences were no greater than one degree. "[31]

IV. · 8. Including the Family in the Rating of Family Functioning

The Scale of Family Functioning is designed to make assessments of social functioning and changes in that functioning on the basis of interview data and interviewer observations. Client views and goals are comprehensively reported in the Profile and are taken into full consideration when the narrative data are coded. Nonetheless, the researcher may wish to obtain a family's own evaluation of the situation, which is at once a more direct and independent assessment than that of the interviewer. The attitudes of family members regarding their common life, values, and goals are significant because they constitute the material from which the helping sciences can gather an understanding of behavior and behavior change. In fact, knowledge about the client's views on treatment, a much neglected area of research, can be of key importance in service planning and execution. Indeed, it has been said again and again that service assessment is well nigh meaningless without obtaining the views of the client who is, after all, the main object of any treatment endeavor.

There are, however, certain problems encountered when attempting to compare a family's evaluation of their own social functioning with that of the researcher's if the comparison is cross-sectional rather than longitudinal. First, there is the requirement that the family and the coder use the same coding

scheme.   It is unrealistic to expect any particular group of families to "buy" the evaluative frame of reference developed here, and
it is equally undesirable to restrict the freedom of the family's independent evaluation by imposing a professional framework upon
them.

These difficulties can be overcome, however, when change
in functioning over time is studied, since change constitutes a modification of the situation, for better or worse, in terms of standards
that are meaningful to the respondent and not necessarily to the
researcher.   Therefore, when examining the family's own evaluation of social functioning the focus should be upon change.

In order to obtain this kind of information from both client
and nonclient families, a schedule was constructed to measure
change in family functioning as perceived by the respondent.   Paral-
leling the Profile of Family Functioning, it contains items organized
by the same areas and sub-categories.   The total number of items,
all of which are structured, or closed, is 49, and their number
per sub-category ranges from 1 to 5.   This schedule is used to
self-evaluate change occurring over a particular time period which
is clearly delineated in the minds of the respondents.   Time may
be defined to the respondents, for example, as that period during
which the family received treatment services of one kind or another;
it may be a period that began with an event which was a landmark
in family history (a wedding, birth of a first child, death of a
family member, a drastic change in the family's economic fortunes,
etc.).   Measurement of change, then, is retrospective, but its
potentially subjective character is mitigated by guidelines along
which change can be rated.   Areas and sub-categories--paralleling
the Profile of Family Functioning--in which movement or change in
functioning may have taken place, and degrees of change--positive,
negative, or zero--are specified in the schedule.   (See schedule
Self-Evaluation of Family Functioning below.)

The schedule data can be statistically analyzed in a number
of ways, depending upon their distribution.   (The five point continuum bears no relationship to the seven levels of family function-

ing discussed above, for it must be remembered that the present schedule deals only with change in, and not the status of, social functioning.) Change as registered by a family's self-evaluation can be analyzed in terms of the five point continuum given in the schedule--if scores are well distributed--or in terms of a simple plus, zero, and negative pattern. If data are heavily skewed further simplification in the form of score dichotomies is indicated, which can be accomplished by combining zero with positive or negative changes. Correlational analysis between the Family Profile and the self-evaluation data may then be carried out by areas and/or sub-categories. At this point the self-evaluation schedule has been employed in two as yet unpublished studies. [32]

The measurement of family functioning can be even further refined by establishing a scheme of evaluation based upon the goals and priorities of the study population. This approach will alleviate the ever present danger of imposing standards of assessment from the outside. To make certain that measurement is completely relevant to each type of family universe, new rating schemes must be devised or existing ones modified to fit each respective population every time there is a new research attempt. In two recent studies, one in Canada and the other in the United States, [33] beginning efforts have been made to devise separate techniques for social workers and clients, appropriate to each, whereby they could assess movement. In both projects, the researchers based their evaluation of client change on broad guidelines for self-rating which did not require a spelling out of the criteria by which movement would be rated.

SELF-EVALUATION OF FAMILY FUNCTIONING

As part of our study of families who have received services, we would like to find out how you think things have changed for you and your family between the time when services were started and when they were terminated (or up to the present, if services are continuing). Please indicate in every area by a circle whether a change occurred in your situation, and if so, how much of a change. If you don't know the answer to the question, or if it is not relevant, circle "Don't Know" or "Not Relevant," whichever is appropriate.

THE SITUATION NOW IS

A.1.	(1) Much Worse	(2) Slightly Worse	(3) No Change	(4) Slightly Better	(5) Much Better	(0) Don't Know	Not Relevant
1. How do you and your husband (wife) get along generally?	W	w	Nc	b	B	?	Nr
2. Has there been any change in how you and your husband (wife) put up with each other's moods?	W	w	Nc	b	B	?	Nr
3. Any change in how you and your husband (wife) discuss problems and share feelings?	W	w	Nc	b	B	?	Nr

THE SITUATION NOW IS

	(1) Much Worse	(2) Slightly Worse	(3) No Change	(4) Slightly Better	(5) Much Better	(0) Don't Know	Not Relevant
4. Any change in how you get along sexually?	W	w	Nc	b	B	?	Nr
5. Any change in the way you and your husband (wife) feel about each other's leisure time activities?		w		b	B	?	Nr
2. / 6. How do you and your husband (wife) get along with your children?	W	w	Nc	b	B	?	Nr
7. Has there been a change in how you feel about your children?	W	w	Nc	b	B	?	Nr
3. / 8. How do the children in your home get along with each other?	W	w	Nc	b	B	?	Nr
4. / 9. Has there been any change in how you and your husband (wife) plan for the future?	W	w	Nc	b	B	?	Nr
10. Any change in how you, as a family, do things together?	W	w	Nc	b	B	?	Nr

THE SITUATION NOW IS

		(1) Much Worse	(2) Slightly Worse	(3) No Change	(4) Slightly Better	(5) Much Better	(0) Don't Know	Not Relevant
11.	Any change in how, you, as a family, "pull together" in times of trouble?	W	w	Nc	b	B	?	Nr
5.	If someone other than your husband (wife), children, or your parents live with you, has there been any change in how all of you have been getting along together?	W	w	Nc	b	B	?	Nr
B.1.	13. Has there been any change in how you feel about yourself?	W	w	Nc	b	B	?	Nr
	14. Do you feel that your dress and general appearance have changed since we first saw you?	W	w	Nc	b	B	?	Nr
	15. Has there been any change in how you get along with people in general?	W	w	Nc	b	B	?	Nr

THE SITUATION NOW IS

		(1) Much Worse	(2) Slightly Worse	(3) No Change	(4) Slightly Better	(5) Much Better	(0) Don't Know	Not Relevant
2.	16. Do you think there has been any change in how your husband (wife) feels about himself (herself) and gets along with people in general?	W	w	Nc	b	B	?	Nr
C.1.	17. Has there been any change in the condition and amount of your children's clothing?	W	w	Nc	b	B	?	Nr
	18. Any change in how you feed and generally take care of your children?	W	w	Nc	b	B	?	Nr
2.	19. Any change in how you and your husband (wife) agree on disciplining the children?	W	w	Nc	b	B	?	Nr
	20. Any change in the way you actually discipline the children?	W	w	Nc	b	B	?	Nr
D.1.	21. Has there been a change in how you get along with your family and your husband's (wife's) family?	W	w	Nc	b	B	?	Nr

THE SITUATION NOW IS

	(1) Much Worse	(2) Slightly Worse	(3) No Change	(4) Slightly Better	(5) Much Better	(0) Don't Know	Not Relevant
22. Has anything changed in how you get along with your neighbors?	W	w	Nc	b	B	?	Nr
23. Any change in satisfaction with the way you spend your free time?	W	w	Nc	b	B	?	Nr
24. Has there been any change in the way you and your husband (wife) participate in clubs, unions, and other organizations?	W	w	Nc	b	B	?	Nr
25. Any change in how you or your husband (wife) feel about belonging to clubs and other organizations?	W	w	Nc	b	B	?	Nr
E.1. 26. Since services started, what changes have there been in your actual cash income?	W	w	Nc	b	B	?	Nr
27. How satisfied are you with your present income as compared to the way you felt about your income when services started?	W	w	Nc	b	B	?	Nr

THE SITUATION NOW IS

		(1) Much Worse	(2) Slightly Worse	(3) No Change	(4) Slightly Better	(5) Much Better	(0) Don't Know	Not Rele-vant
28.	How does your present income, compared to previous income, meet your actual needs?	W	w	Nc	b	B	?	Nr
2. 29.	If you, or your husband (wife) are employed, has there been a change in job satisfaction?	W	w	Nc	b	B	?	Nr
30.	Is that job more suited to your or your husband's (wife's) abilities than before?	W	w	Nc	b	B	?	Nr
3. 31.	Has there been a change in how you and your husband (wife) agree on how money ought to be spent?	W	w	Nc	b	B	?	Nr
32.	If you have any debts, is there any change in how you are able to meet payment on these debts?	W	w	Nc	b	B	?	Nr
33.	What kind of money managers or budgeters are you now as compared to then?	W	w	Nc	b	B	?	Nr

THE SITUATION NOW IS

		(1) Much Worse	(2) Slightly Worse	(3) No Change	(4) Slightly Better	(5) Much Better	(0) Don't Know	Not Relevant
F.1.	34. Any change in the kind of apartment or house which you now occupy?	W	w	Nc	b	B	?	Nr
	35. Is the neighborhood you live in better or worse now?	W	w	Nc	b	B	?	Nr
	36. Has there been a change in the quantity or quality of your household furniture and furnishings?	W	w	Nc	b	B	?	Nr
2.	37. Has there been a change in your (or your wife's) house-keeping habits?	W	w	Nc	b	B	?	Nr
	38. Have you changed in the way you (or your wife) serve and plan meals?	W	w	Nc	b	B	?	Nr
	39. Has there been a change in the ease with which you (or your wife) perform your household chores?	W	w	Nc	b	B	?	Nr

THE SITUATION NOW IS

		(1) Much Worse	(2) Slightly Worse	(3) No Change	(4) Slightly Better	(5) Much Better	(0) Don't Know	Not Relevant
G.1.	40. How is your health and that of members of your immediate family now as compared to the time services began?	W	w	Nc	b	B	?	Nr
2.	41. Have there been changes in the way you take care of your own and your family's health needs?	W	w	Nc	b	B	?	Nr
	42. Any change in the manner in which you get medical and dental checkups or keep appointments?	W	w	Nc	b	B	?	Nr
H.1.	43. Has there been any change in your feeling about the social worker who has been serving you?	W	w	Nc	b	B	?	Nr
	44. Has there been any change in the way you are able to work together with your social worker?	W	w	Nc	b	B	?	Nr

THE SITUATION NOW IS

		(1) Much Worse	(2) Slightly Worse	(3) No Change	(4) Slightly Better	(5) Much Better	(0) Don't Know	Not Relevant
I.1.	45. Has there been a change in how you feel about schools and education for your children?	W	w	Nc	b	B	?	Nr
2.	46. Has there been any change in your church or synagogue-going habits?	W	w	Nc	b	B	?	Nr
3.	47. Are there any changes in the way you use health resources, such as clinics, private doctors, hospitals?	W	w	Nc	b	B	?	Nr
4.	48. How do you now use social agencies, as compared to when services started?	W	w	Nc	b	B	?	Nr
5.	49. Has there been a change in how you use recreational agencies?	W	w	Nc	b	B	?	Nr

V. MEASURING COMMUNITY FUNCTIONING

V. 1. Introduction

Before the turn of the century, American social work was
already making attempts to establish community wide practice. The
Charity Organization Societies, confronted by a multiplicity of efforts all aimed at raising funds and providing services, sought to
bring order out of the confusion by establishing a measure of coordination among agencies. However, community organization as
a differentiated method of social work practice was not born until
the 1920's. Early formulations were broad in nature and centered
on "reconstruction of the small community ... sustaining a democratic process, involving the citizen and the expert at the grass
roots level, to make a viable creative entity out of the community. "[1]
By the 1940's and 50's the chief emphasis in community organization had shifted to the coordination of welfare services to meet human need. Consequently, fund raising and work with community
welfare councils became significant foci in training community organization practitioners.

More recently there has been a further shift, a movement
toward an institutional approach in which social work in general
and community organization in particular devote themselves to meeting the basic needs of the total population instead of confining themselves to the socially handicapped. Community organization in this
context is concerned with social organization, power structure, and
social change. This approach makes it possible for social work to
utilize the community theory and research which come from the
disciplines of sociology and social psychology.

In spite of social work's abiding concern with community
needs and problems, there has been comparatively little research
done on these subjects. [2] Priority of needs studies, much in vogue
during the 1950's, [3] were eventually abandoned under the impact of

152

a nation-wide movement which sought to give the consumer of services a greater share in determining their nature.

As was suggested at the beginning of this manual, the study
of community functioning is an attempt to utilize a common theoretical dimension in examining the needs and problems of different units
of society. The community is a most significant subject of study
for social work because it represents the larger social context, as
it were, within which other objects of social work intervention--in-
dividuals, families, social and recreational groups, institutions,
etc. --come to life, develop, and function. Assessment of the behavior or functioning of these other units is incomplete without
knowledge of the functioning of the larger system. The measurement focus of the instrument to be presented is need for professional intervention. A discussion of the theoretical background for
the endeavor follows in the next section. Unlike the St. Paul Scale
of Family Functioning, the Community Functioning Scale is a new
product which has been subjected only to limited methodological
testing as shown below.

V. 2. Theoretical Underpinnings

Before attempting to discuss the technique of measurement
there is need to give further consideration to some of the theoretical premises underlying the evaluative approach.   The development
of theoretical frameworks that are useful for empirical study have
been retarded by the vast number of definitions the term community
has been given in the sociological literature.   Because of this di-
versity in meaning a broad definition of community such as was
evolved by Roland L. Warren is probably most useful, at least for
research such as this with an applied or technology-oriented focus.
Warren defined the community as "that combination of social units
and systems which performs the major social function having locality
relevance."[4] This definition conveniently avoids the problems of
specifying size, geographic space, length and degree of contact,
association of units and systems, and so forth.   The community,
according to Warren, represents an "organization of social activities to afford people daily local access to those broad areas of activity which are necessary in day-to-day living."[5] He then proceeds
to classify activities in terms of five major functions which are
said to have locality relevance: (1) production-distribution-consump-
tion; (2) socialization; (3) social control; (4) social participation;
and (5) mutual support.[6]

This manual follows Warren in making functions a central
concept around which data are to be organized.   At the same time
it should be remembered that the function-focused approach is part
of a broader theoretical stance, shown in Chapter II, which builds
upon the social systems concept.   Functions, as stated earlier,
are the processes which contribute to the continuity and ordered
change of the system (see Chapter III).   The three basic systems
goals of autonomy, integration, and viability have been shown to
be applicable to the community as well as to the family and,
presumably, to other social systems.

As a social system the community differs from most others
in the large number and different kinds of sub-systems which it

encompasses.   This led Edward Moe to call it a system of systems. [7]
Warren, however, makes clear that the main difference between community and other systems is not the existence of numerous and diverse sub-systems but rather the way in which these relate to one
another. [8]   In contrast to formal organizations, the sub-systems in
the community are not rationally or deliberately related to each
other but simply coexist, for the most part, meeting a vast variety
of needs.   Some organizations and institutions such as city councils,
municipal committees and departments, etc. , are, of course, centrally connected.   Many others, however, exist only in relation to
the needs, interests, and goals of some of the community's citizens
or groups and have no connection to the community system as a
whole.   Other sub-systems, such as churches or banks, are part
of a hierarchical and centrally organized structure whose center of
operations is entirely outside the community.

      Sub-systems of the family, such as parents, siblings, mother-
daughter alliances, etc. , can be readily identified and their relationship to the family system can be easily assessed.   Community sub-
systems are exceedingly variable with respect to structure, function,
goals, and purposes, making it virtually impossible to study community functioning from the vantage point of tasks and functions. [9]
Therefore, the study of community functioning outlined here does
not attempt to directly evaluate the actual sub-systems or their
functions but concerns itself instead with the way the performance
of some basic tasks is viewed by the community.   The community's
perception of the performance of tasks is a reflection, as it were,
of the way the community sub-systems are functioning.   The functions of the sub-systems may be referred to--as was done in the
family functioning framework--as the functional prerequisites for
the community system.

      There is yet another reason for refraining from a direct
assessment of sub-systems in the study of community functioning.
Their goals and functions, unlike those of parents or children, are
not only infinitely variable but also poorly defined.   It would be
most difficult to reach any consensus on the "socially expected
functions" of such diverse groups as chambers of commerce,

P. T. A. 's, boards of education, anti-poverty corporations, recreation councils, churches, etc. The present approach does not disregard the actual community sub-systems; it merely avoids studying them directly and postulates instead the existence of certain universal community structures, such as the labor market, welfare organizations, educational services, political parties, whose functioning can be evaluated indirectly through the attitudes of individuals in the community. These structures undergird the functional prerequisites of the system which enable the community to render the services needed by its population.

The postulation of community sub-systems and the indirect measurement of their functioning serves a most important purpose in this study. Based upon the notion that there are certain universal functions that must be performed to meet the basic needs of any and all populations in every community, no matter how large or small, homogeneous or diversified, the present approach rates a community by whether or not, in one form or another, the functions have been carried out without investigating whether sub-systems have actually been established to fulfill them.

Ideally, research on community functioning ought to be directly measuring the functioning of its component parts--as was done in relation to the family--through observation, questioning, examining records, and so forth. But in a structure as complex as a community, small as it might be, that would be a most formidable undertaking, calling for a very large investment in time and funds. Alternatively, the approach taken here of indirect measurement examines the extent to which services and resources deemed universally needed (at least in this society) meet the basic needs of community members. Like the study of the family, one of the underlying assumptions of community research is that the systems function to assure their own continuity, and this relies in turn upon the achievement of their basic goals, defined earlier as autonomy, integration, and viability. Central to these are the needs of their constituents for material, biological, social, and emotional well-being. Therefore, a key indicant for assessing the quality of

the community's social functioning is the extent to which services
and resources satisfy the population. Community functioning, when
operationalized, reads the judgment of community members as to
the adequacy or inadequacy of the provisions for services, resources,
and opportunities, which fall into two basic conceptual groupings:
Primary provisions for survival, maintenance of minimum level of
social functioning, and basic socialization; and Secondary provisions
to achieve social participation, social control, mobility, social and
political and cultural expression, and adequate instrumental living
arrangements. Primary and secondary provisions are not sharply
divided but differ mainly by degree of presumed urgency. The
categorization rests upon the assumption that, in American society,
income, employment, shelter, and social security meet more funda-
mental needs than social participation or social control, insofar as
they refer to an individual's chance to live a satisfactory life. It
must be borne in mind, nevertheless, that under certain conditions
secondary provisions may become more salient than certain primary
ones. For instance, social control in the form of police protection
may be more important than housing to a resident of the inner city
with its high crime rate. Or the absence of public transportation
(instrumental needs) may pose a more serious problem to the low-
income resident than poor schools (primary socialization), for if he
cannot afford a private car and is unable to reach his job by means
of public transportation, the family's livelihood is threatened. However, this writer argues that, by and large, primary provisions
as identified in this study are more directly associated with the
issue of survival than secondary ones.

     The relationship between the basic goals of social systems
and primary and secondary provisions to meet population needs in
the community system is shown in Chart III.

     As the chart shows, provisions to meet the needs of popula-
tion are, for the most part, integrative in nature, in the sense that
they serve to unify and harmonize the constituent elements of the
system while furthering its instrumental and expressive aims. Provisions for social control, however, such as protecting citizens

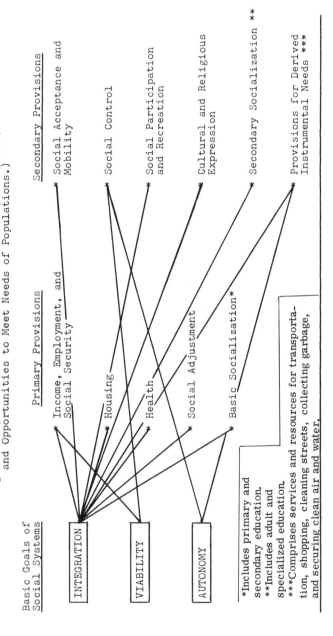

CHART III. CONCEPTUAL FRAMEWORK FOR EVALUATING COMMUNITY FUNCTIONING

Functional Prerequisites of the Community System
(Organized by Areas of Provisions for Services, Resources,
and Opportunities to Meet Needs of Populations.)

Basic Goals of
Social Systems

Primary Provisions

Secondary Provisions

Income, Employment, and
Social Security

Housing

Health

Social Adjustment

Basic Socialization*

Social Acceptance and
Mobility

Social Control

Social Participation
and Recreation

Cultural and Religious
Expression

Secondary Socialization **

Provisions for Derived
Instrumental Needs ***

INTEGRATION

VIABILITY

AUTONOMY

*Includes primary and
secondary education.
**Includes adult and
specialized education.
***Comprises services and resources for transporta-
tion, shopping, cleaning streets, collecting garbage,
and securing clean air and water.

against hazards and providing security to residents in times of crisis, enable the system to remain viable, while other forms of social control and provisions for derived instrumental needs, such as transportation and shopping facilities, enable the system to be autonomous.

In relating community functions or provisions for services, resources, and opportunities to the concept of need, we are focusing on some of the basic concerns of social work practice. Need denotes a demand for gratification on one or more levels of behavior, biological, psychological, or social. If that gratification is not forthcoming, need may be said to prevail (it is sometimes also referred to as unmet need) and is generally considered to constitute a type of social problem. [10]

Need is a key concept, a term used by all methods of social work. Whether in casework, group work, or community organization, the practitioner is confronted with the task of identifying the needs of his clientele and then dealing with them according to their urgency, their priority for fulfillment, their potential for being satisfied by direct or indirect means, and the possible alternatives to their gratification. Needs are usually seen as the properties of an individual, family, or other small group. Societal values and norms, by contrast, provide the framework within which needs may be judged as being amenable to satisfaction. [11]

When relating need to the total community, the concept continues to apply to individuals and small groups but we focus upon the extent to which it appears in the total system. Wide prevalence of need, need which is shared by most individuals or small groups within a given system and is, therefore, statistically definable, can be termed need-consensus.

It is possible for need and need-consensus to exist in an infinite number of behavior and functioning areas, so that categorizing needs would be a very ambitious undertaking. Therefore, for purposes of measurement we have identified a series of areas within which services, resources, and opportunities are made available to members of a community with an eye toward meeting a variety of biological, psychological, social, and material needs.

The framework of categories is basically institutional, although it differentiates, as was pointed out earlier, between provisions (primary) related to meeting survival needs and provisions (secondary) aimed at satisfying needs assumed to be less crucial for human existence.

If need-consensus exists in a substantial number of areas of service provision, it is a sign of poor community functioning, signifying failure to meet the basic needs of a population. Need-consensus does not fix blame or responsibility for such failure for it does not identify which structure or sub-structure was charged with meeting specific needs. There are, indeed, striking variations among communities with regard to the allocation of responsibility to external agencies, institutions, organizations, etc. The presence of need-consensus merely indicates that within a given community certain needs have not been met, and in this sense the community may be said to be malfunctioning. The question of identifying the particular sub-systems which failed in their operations is a statutory one. On the American scene, the responsibility for the welfare of community residents is shared by the municipality, the county, the state, and the Federal Government. The relative contributions of each differ widely, depending on a number of factors--size of community, local resources, the legislative framework of each type (federal to municipal) of authority. Only in the broadest sense can community malfunctioning be identified with community failure, namely, if we accept the assumption that political incorporation or self-government carries with it the moral and/or administrative responsibility to meet the needs of constituents.

A point made by this writer in an earlier paper must be stressed here, namely, that "the goal of community functioning as formulated here is not an absolute state of performance, as implied in the concept of Utopia, but a situation where the actions and activities of the system meet the needs of its members."[12] Need-consensus reflects a gap, as it were, between the requirements for the welfare of residents and the actual ways in which they are met. Need and need-consensus are not absolutes but

properties related to the psycho-social characteristics of the population. A crucial factor determining need are people's expectations,
which in turn have been shaped by past experience, prevailing standards and norms, and available opportunities. The gap between requirements and resources is also relative in character because its
magnitude is determined by the nature of a population's needs.

Two possible approaches could be used to measure the manner in which residents of communities have their needs met: (1)
Determining the needs of community members and obtaining a personal assessment from each resident on the way in which his specific needs are being met by community services and resources; and
(2) Gathering the views of community residents on the ways in which
community members have their needs met, regardless of whether
they themselves are actually experiencing any one need.

While it may seem that the first approach is the more precise and logical because it bases evaluation on direct personal experience, it requires an a priori determination of what each person's needs are--a most formidable undertaking. Age, sex, occupation, place of residence provide some very sketchy guidelines indicating an individual's need for services and resources. They are
rough indeed, for within each category of community membership
need is also determined by intelligence, state of health, degree of
social adjustment, and so forth. To make this first approach fea-
sible it would be necessary to have the assessment of need-meeting
be preceded by a comprehensive need study. Such an expensive
and time consuming undertaking would be justified if we had conclusive evidence that people are able to provide more valid data regarding the ways in which their own needs are being met than about
the manner in which the needs of others are being satisfied. Lacking such evidence, the first approach, which would require the use
of large samples in order to secure representatives from population groupings reflecting every kind of need, was abandoned. It
was decided to adopt the second approach which relies on an analysis of the responses of each community member regarding every
need for services and resources that had been identified in the

study. To guard against meaningless answers respondents have
been encouraged to check the item "I know nothing about the subject" whenever they lack information about the way specific needs
are being met.

To summarize, the present research studies community
functioning by securing the responses of community residents--or
a sample of residents--regarding the adequacy of basic provisions
of services, resources, and opportunities to meet the needs of the
population. We assume that meaningful responses can be obtained
from most adults who have been living in a community and have
been witness to the ways in which various needs are being met.
Residents of a community may experience the functioning of services directly, as they or members of their families are served by
educational, health, or welfare agencies, or indirectly, as relatives,
friends, and neighbors share their experiences with them, or as
they learn about others from the news media.

Validity in the evaluation of community functioning resides
essentially in a correct assessment of the attitudes of residents
about the way needs are being met. What is being evaluated is
the reciprocal relationship between needs and resources, in other
words, the system's ability to cope with such need as may be found
in diverse areas of human functioning. Objection may be raised to
the fact that such a definition of community functioning constitutes
a highly subjective property. This subjectivity, however, does not
of itself diminish validity as long as it is understood that we are
not seeking to measure the actual organizational effectiveness or
quality of services but the beliefs of the local population. It is
not farfetched to assume that the beliefs are correlated with service
quality when there is a need for services. However, such a corre-
lation is not crucial to the success of the present evaluative endeavor
and might appropriately become the subject of a separate study.
Community functioning, as operationalized here, takes on its major
significance as a variable which informs the researcher as to the
population's views about the relationship between resources and
needs. This variable represents a social fact that is of importance

for those who plan and render, as well as for those who receive, services.

Chart III, presented above, furnished the conceptual framework of the provisions for services, resources, and opportunities. It is organized into two area groupings, primary and secondary, according to the assumed urgency of needs, and into eleven areas of services, resources, and opportunities for meeting these population needs. Each area is composed of several items, ranging from two to ten in number, making a total of 42 items. These items grouped by areas are given below:

A. PRIMARY PROVISIONS

1. Income, Employment, and Social Security

> Financial assistance for those who cannot work and have
> no other source of income, or do not earn enough

> Unemployment insurance

> Workmen's compensation

> Social Security for the retired

> Jobs for all who are able to work

> Job finding, placement, and training

2. Housing

> Low cost public housing

> Middle-income housing

> Less costly private housing

3. Basic Socialization

> Schools for children at the elementary and high school
> level

> Special classes and services for children with learning
> problems

> Job training for those who lack skills and education to
> hold a decent job

4. <u>Health</u>

   Low cost or free services of doctors and dentists, hospitals, clinics, and baby-keep-well stations

   Private services of doctors, dentists, hospitals, and clinics

   Comprehensive medical insurance

5. <u>Social Adjustment</u>

   Counseling and guidance services for people and families with problems

   Treatment services and institutions for the mentally ill, alcoholics, drug addicts, and other seriously maladjusted persons

   Facilities for children placed away from their homes, such as institutions, foster homes, etc.

   Nursing homes for the elderly in need of constant care

   Social and recreational services for the elderly

   Rehabilitation services for the physically handicapped

   Special educational and vocational services for the mentally retarded and brain damaged

   Homemaker services for mothers out of the home

   Day care centers and nurseries for the children of working mothers

   Parole, probation, and other services for delinquent youths and adults

B. SECONDARY PROVISIONS

   6. <u>Social Acceptance and Mobility</u>

      A chance for everyone to be fully accepted, regardless of race, color, or creed

      Opportunities for all to get ahead economically and socially

   7. <u>Social Control</u>

      Protection against personal hazards and damage of all

kinds through the services of the fire department,
police department, courts, etc.

Legal protection regardless of ability to pay legal fees

Opportunities for political expression through voting,
political organization, and other forms of democratic
process

Opportunities to change things with which you are dissatisfied at the municipal level, by talking or writing to
officials, staging protests, etc.

8. Social Participation and Recreation

Clubs, neighborhood centers and other organizations of-
fering social, recreational, and educational programs

Recreational facilities such as parks, playgrounds, swimming pools, sports fields, etc.

9. Secondary Socialization

Provisions for higher and specialized education

Adult education courses and programs

10. Cultural and Religious Expression

Opportunities for cultural and artistic pursuits

Opportunities for religious expression and participation

11. Provisions for Derived Instrumental Needs

Transportation Facilities (public or private) for getting
to work, for shopping and social occasions

Shopping within easy reach

Efficient garbage collection and sewage facilities

Cleaning and maintenance of roads and sidewalks

Clean air and water

This selection of items was accomplished by two preliminary
studies: the first sought to identify issues of concern to the community welfare planner, [13] and the second compared the attitudes
of those who plan services with those who consume them. [14] In the

course of these studies it became clear that elite groups and rank
and file members of the community do not necessarily agree upon
social welfare needs.   The two studies led to the creation of a list
of items that appeared relevant for respondents living in a medium-
sized urban community.   Further testing and modification of the
items was brought about by a community needs and action study with
a random sample of young urban families in a metropolitan community. [15]   The final scale product presented here is, of course,
not truly final.   It is the array of provisions identified as meeting
common human needs in an urban seaboard area.   Other parts of
the United States may reflect the same type of need structure and
may, therefore, be researched effectively with the aid of the present instrument or they may have different need structures making
instrument modifications necessary.

In concluding this section there is need to emphasize that
the study of community functioning by way of assessing provisions
for services, resources, and opportunities to meet need is research
into the system's performance, measured against a hypothetical
model of service structure which meets universal (within this cultural setting) human needs.   Whether each one of these needs is
present or whether the community has established an appropriate
structure for meeting them is not here the issue.   What the research sets out to determine is the nature of the reciprocal relationship between requirements for services and the community's
provisions to satisfy them.   The methodology for studying this relationship utilizes the views of consumers or potential consumers
of services, for they reflect unambiguously the success or failure
of the community welfare enterprise.

V. 3. Rating Procedure and Collection of Data Covering Related Variables

The study of community functioning, in contrast to that of family functioning, uses a precoded instrument which obviates the need for coders and rating criteria. Responses to the community functioning questionnaire are given on a four point Likert type continuum. Respondents are asked to check whether, in relation to various kinds of needs, they consider services, resources, and opportunities as being

(1) Adequate as they are or not needed;

(2) Less than adequate, some improvement needed;

(3) Less than adequate, great improvement needed;

(4) Entirely lacking or wholly inadequate, urgently needed.

Forty-two questionnaire items are grouped by the conceptual categories presented above without any headings being shown in the instrument itself. The grouping was not seen as promoting a respondent acquiescent set, since conceptually related items in each area are yet quite distinct from one another and require the interviewee to respond to discrete, specific stimuli. The response category (5), "I know nothing about the subject," is designed to reduce the likelihood of gathering opinions on a need-service dimension with which the respondent is unfamiliar.

The schedule presented here allows for the gathering of some data beyond the 42 items (numbers 7 - 48) covering the provision of services, resources, and opportunities dimension. These data, the collection of which is optional for the researcher concerned exclusively with exploring social welfare (in the broadest sense) aspects of community functioning, cover a number of demographic and attitudinal variables which are theoretically relevant to the study of community provisions to meet population needs.

Demographic variables covering age, sex, marital status, number of children, education, occupation, religion, race, and length of residence in the community are dealt with by schedule

items 60-70. Item number 80 permits the coding, according to
any number of systems to be selected by the researcher, of type
of socio-economic status of respondent. Schedule items 1-7 are
set aside for identifying the respondent, his neighborhood (optional)
and the particular community in which the study was done.

Social and political participation and use of community health
and welfare services are dealt with by items 71 to 79. Information
about these subjects would appear to be relevant when exploring the
connection between attitude toward the existing service structure and
involvement in and/or with community organizations and agencies.
It can be argued that such involvement is likely to affect a person's
perception of a community's functioning and modify his attitudes toward the adequacy of services and resources. Of course one's
perception can be affected in two ways: the volunteer worker, especially one who is a member of an elite group, may see the performance of community services in a more favorable light than does
the uninvolved person. Use of agencies rendering high quality services may have the same effect. By contrast, experience with an
agency which provides poor services is likely to color negatively
the views of a respondent toward the local service structure.

Another dimension covered in the questionnaire, "measures
that are likely to get results to the extent that changes in the service structure are considered desirable" (items 49 - 59), can be
viewed as both an independent and dependent variable in the study
of community functioning. This dimension is made up of items denoting different means to attain desired goals, ranging from the
conventional and generally accepted--such as voting and writing letters to legislators--to the innovative and deviant: organizing new
groups and holding demonstrations, both violent and nonviolent.

It is hypothesized that a person's beliefs regarding his
chances of bringing about desired changes in the service structure
tend to color his views about the quality of services. Belief in
the efficacy of conventional and nondeviant methods is thought to
foster more favorable opinions about the adequacy of services relative to need. Correlatively, a negative attitude toward the service

structure is likely to give rise to the advocacy of innovative and deviant means of effecting change.   Whatever the actual nature of the postulated causal relationship, the demonstration of an existing association between the two variables can be of considerable signi- ficance for service planning which, if it is to be effective, must address itself to the social and political aspirations of the population.

Whereas coding of the community functioning data is already built into the structure of the scale and requires no further rating efforts, the analysis of the data presents a series of options de- termined, at least in part, by· the service need response patterns of the population tested.   Heterogeneous response distributions, which approximate the normal curve on most items, make analysis by each response item on the five point continuum.possible, espec- ially when the study comprises sizeable samples.   More homo- geneous distributions require decisions to group responses tricho- tomously or dichotomously, the latter being a statistical accommoda- tion to minimum data variability.   Although the conceptual scheme presented above has provided a useful framework for collecting items and ordering them preliminarily in the analysis, the use of large, representative study samples should afford an opportunity to carry out scale refinement and simplification by factor analysis and related methods.

The questionnaire for collecting data on community function- ing is given below.   The schedule has been pre-coded for immediate IBM card punching and computer processing.   Appropriate coding systems will have to be selected for items 66, 67, and 80.

COMMUNITY STUDY QUESTIONNAIRE

The Rutgers University Graduate School of Social
Work is doing a study on community needs and community
action. The purpose of this study is to get a better idea
about the needs and wishes of the population with regard
to the social services of the community. A further goal
of the study is to convey to community leaders and planners the views of citizens on the subject of social services, in the hope that the findings of the study will contribute toward better planning and programming.

To make this study possible we are requesting
about half an hour of your time to answer some questions
on need for services and ways of bringing about desired
changes in the services. The basic question we are asking you is this:

HOW SATISFACTORY ARE EACH ONE OF THE COM-
MUNITY SERVICES, RESOURCES, AND OPPORTUNITIES
LISTED BELOW?

The services, resources, and opportunities listed
here are generally considered important to the health and
welfare of the community. Some are provided by the community itself, others are furnished by the county, the
state, the federal government or local and national volun-
tary organizations. Regardless of who provides the services, we should like you to express your thoughts and
feelings about each type of service, resource, and opportunity. Which of the five answers below best represents
your own opinion on each subject?

Services, resources, and opportunities are:

(1) Adequate as they are or are not needed;

(2) Less than adequate, some improvement needed;

(3) Less than adequate, great improvement needed;

(4) Entirely lacking or wholly inadequate, urgently
     needed;

(5) I really do not know anything about that par-
     ticular subject.

In selecting one answer or another you should be
guided by what you believe the situation is in your community regardless of whether or not you and your family
needs or has ever used such a service. Your reply will
of course be influenced by any experience you may have

had with the service, but beyond that your opinion is most likely to be determined by the experiences of relatives, friends, acquaintances, and neighbors, and by what you hear on the radio, see on T. V. or read in the newspaper or in magazines. Regardless of the source of information it is your point-of-view we are interested in.

In reading the items you may say that you do not have all the pertinent information. That may be correct, but none of us has all the pertinent information. We simply form an opinion on the basis of what we have learned. To know your opinion is very important to us. At the same time we wish to assure you that all information you give us will be treated with complete confidentiality.

Finally, one last point. Before selecting one of the answers consider first whether there is need in the community for a given service. If there is need for a given service your answer is determined by how well the services, resources, or opportunities meet that need. If there is no need for a service, the proper answer is the first one, "services are adequate as they are or are not needed. "

In the hope that we have succeeded in conveying to you the goals of our study we are asking you to check one but only one of the answers to each item listed below. Select answer number (5) only when you know absolutely nothing about the service mentioned. Repeating the question again we should like you to tell us:

HOW SATISFACTORY ARE EACH ONE OF THE SERVICES, RESOURCES, AND OPPORTUNITIES IN YOUR COMMUNITY?

Please check items in the appropriate column, beginning with question 7 on the next page.

```
            DO NOT FILL IN
    ┌─────────────────────────────────┐
    │ (For research coder only)       │
    │                                 │
    │  1. _____  Community          │
    │                                 │
    │  2. _____  I.D. Number        │
    │                                 │
    │  3. _____                     │
    │                                 │
    │  4. _____                     │
    │                                 │
    │  5. _____                     │
    │                                 │
    │  6. _____                     │
    │                                 │
    └─────────────────────────────────┘
```

	SERVICES, RESOURCES AND OPPORTUNITIES				
	(1) Adequate as they are or not needed	(2) Some improvement needed	(3) Great improvement needed	(4) Entirely lacking or wholly inadequate; urgently needed	(5) I know nothing about the subject
7. Financial assistance for those who can't work and have no other source of income or don't earn enough					
8. Unemployment insurance					
9. Workmen's compensation					
10. Social Security for the retired					
11. Jobs for all that are able to work					
12. Job finding, placement, and training					
13. Low cost public housing					
14. Middle-income housing					
15. Less costly private housing					
16. Schools for children at the elementary and high school level					

SERVICES, RESOURCES AND OPPORTUNITIES				
	(1) Adequate as they are or not needed	(2) Some improvement needed	(3) Great improvement needed	(4) Entirely lacking or wholly inadequate; urgently needed	(5) I know nothing about the subject
17. Special classes and services for children with learning problems					
18. Job training for those who lack skills and education to hold a decent job					
19. Low cost or free services of doctors and dentists, hospitals, clinics, and baby-keep-well stations					
20. Private services of doctors, dentists, hospitals, and clinics					
21. Comprehensive medical insurance					
22. Counseling and guidance services for people and families with problems					
23. Treatment services and institutions for the mentally ill, alcoholic, drug addict and other seriously maladjusted persons					

SERVICES, RESOURCES AND OPPORTUNITIES	(1) Adequate as they are or not needed	(2) Some improvement needed	(3) Great improvement needed	(4) Entirely Lacking or wholly inadequate; urgently needed	(5) I know nothing about the subject
24. Facilities for children placed away from their homes, such as institutions, foster homes, etc.					
25. Nursing homes for the elderly in need of constant care					
26. Social and recreational services for the elderly					
27. Rehabilitation services for the physically handicapped					
28. Special educational and vocational services for the mentally retarded and brain damaged					
29. Homemaker services for mothers out of the home					
30. Day care centers and nurseries for the children of working mothers					

	SERVICES, RESOURCES AND OPPORTUNITIES				
	(1) Adequate as they are or not needed	(2) Some improvement needed	(3) Great improvement needed	(4) Entirely Lacking or wholly inadequate; urgently needed	(5) I know nothing about the subject
31. Parole, probation, and other services for delinquent youths as well as adults					
32. A chance for everyone to be fully accepted regardless of race, color or creed					
33. Opportunities for all to get ahead economically and socially					
34. Protection against personal hazards and damage of all kinds through the services of the fire department, police department, courts, etc.					
35. Legal protection regardless of ability to pay legal fees					

	(1) Adequate as they are or not needed	(2) Some improvement needed	(3) Great improvement needed	(4) Entirely Lacking or wholly inadequate; urgently needed	(5) I know nothing about the subject
	SERVICES, RESOURCES AND OPPORTUNITIES				
36. Opportunities for political expression, through voting, political organization, and other forms of democratic process					
37. Opportunities to change things with which you are dissatisfied at the municipal level by talking or writing to officials, staging protests, etc.					
38. Clubs, neighborhood centers and other organizations offering social, recreational, and educational programs					
39. Recreational facilities such as parks, playgrounds, swimming pools, sports fields, etc.					
40. Provisions for higher and specialized education					
41. Adult education courses and programs					

| SERVICES, RESOURCES AND OPPORTUNITIES | | | | |
(1) Adequate as they are or not needed	(2) Some improvement needed	(3) Great improvement needed	(4) Entirely Lacking or wholly inadequate; urgently needed	(5) I know nothing about the subject
42. Opportunities for cultural and artistic pursuits				
43. Opportunities for religious expression and participation				
44. Transportation facilities (public or private) for getting to work, for shopping and social occasions				
45. Shopping within easy reach				
46. Efficient garbage collection and sewage facilities				
47. Cleaning and maintenance of roads and sidewalks				
48. Clean air and water				

Family and Community Functioning

To the extent that you believe changes in services, resources, and opportunities in your community are needed, which of the measures listed below is most likely to get results?

	(1) Generally gets results	(2) Sometimes gets results	(3) Seldom gets results	(4) I don't know
49. Letters to legislators, city and government officials				
50. Phone calls to legislators, city and government officials				
51. Personal visits to City Hall legislators, other officials				
52. Obtaining Legal Help				
53. Organizing neighborhood groups or groups of interested people				
54. Action through existing groups, like church groups, clubs, unions, political parties, action groups				
55. Newspaper publicity and other forms of publicity				
56. Non-violent demonstrations				
57. Violent demonstrations				

	(1) Generally gets results	(2) Sometimes gets results	(3) Seldom gets results	(4) I don't know
58. Using <u>influential</u> people with pull				
59. <u>Voting</u>				

In conclusion, we would appreciate a little information about yourself, not to identify you as a person, but rather to enable us to relate the views you expressed to your social characteristics.

60. Your age
(1) _____ Under 18
(2) _____ 18 – 25
(3) _____ 26 – 35
(4) _____ 36 – 45
(5) _____ 46 – 55
(6) _____ 56 – 65
(7) _____ 66 – 75
(8) _____ 76 and over
(BL) _____ Not known

61. Sex
(1) _____ Male
(2) _____ Female

62. Marital Status
(1) _____ Single
(2) _____ Married
(3) _____ Widowed
(4) _____ Divorced
(5) _____ Separated
(BL) _____ N.K. (Not Known)

63. Number of children   (1)_____ None

                          (2)_____ One

                          (3)_____ Two

                          (4)_____ Three

                          (5)_____ Four

                          (6)_____ Five

                          (7)_____ Six

                          (8)_____ Seven

                          (9)_____ Eight or more

                          (0)_____ Not applicable

                          (BL)_____ N. K.

64. Number of years of school completed

Yourself   65. Your spouse

(1)_____   Under 7 years of school   (1)_____

(2)_____   7-9 years of school   (2)_____

(3)_____   10-11 years of school   (3)_____

(4)_____   High school graduate   (4)_____

(5)_____   1-3 years of college (also business   (5)_____
            school)

(6)_____   Four year college graduate   (6)_____

(7)_____   Professional (M.A., M.S., M.E., M.D.,   (7)_____
            Ph.D., Ed.D., M.S.W., L.L.B., D.D., etc.)

(0)_____   Special schools attended beyond   (0)_____
            eighth grade

(BL)_____   Not applicable or not known   (BL)_____

Occupation (give job title, type of organization you
work for and describe briefly what you are doing. If retired
or unemployed list the last job).

66. Your own   67. Your spouse

_____   _____

_____   _____

_____   _____

_____   _____

DO NOT FILL IN

Codes for items. (For research coder only)

66. (1)_____   67. (1)_____
    (2)_____   (2)_____
    (3)_____   (3)_____
    (4)_____   (4)_____
    (5)_____   (5)_____
    (6)_____   (6)_____
    (7)_____   (7)_____
    (8)_____   (8)_____
    (9)_____   (9)_____
    (0)_____ Not Applicable   (0)_____ Not Applicable
    (BL)_____ N.K.   (BL)_____ N.K.

68. Religion (1)_____ Catholic   (4)_____ Other
              (2)_____ Protestant   (5)_____ None
              (3)_____ Jewish   (BL)_____ N.K.

69. Race   (1)_____ Black   (4)_____ Other
              (2)_____ White   (BL)_____ N.K.
              (3)_____ Puerto Rican

70. Length of time you have lived in the community

(1)_____ Less than a year
(2)_____ One year to two years
(3)_____ More than two years to three years
(4)_____ More than three years to four years
(5)_____ More than four years to five years
(6)_____ More than five years to ten years
(7)_____ More than ten years to fifteen years
(8)_____ More than fifteen years to twenty years
(9)_____ More than twenty years to thirty years
(0)_____ More than thirty years
(BL)_____ N. K.

    Number of clubs or organizations, if any, to which you
and your spouse belong (do not include political party, church
or union membership but do list church clubs, union clubs,
and professional associations).

71. Yourself   72. Your spouse

(1)_____   None   (1)_____
(2)_____   One   (2)_____
(3)_____   Two   (3)_____
(4)_____   Three   (4)_____
(5)_____   Four   (5)_____
(6)_____   Five   (6)_____
(7)_____   Six or more   (7)_____
(0)_____   Not Applicable   (0)_____
(BL)_____   N.K.   (BL)_____

    Do you or your spouse hold office in one or more clubs
or organizations (not including political party, union or
church)?

73. Yourself   74. Your spouse

(1)_____   Not an officer   (1)_____
(2)_____   In one club or organization   (2)_____
(3)_____   In two   (3)_____
(4)_____   In three   (4)_____
(5)_____   In four   (5)_____
(6)_____   In five   (6)_____
(7)_____   In six or more   (7)_____
(0)_____   Not Applicable (belongs to   (0)_____
                     no club)
(BL)_____   N.K.   (BL)_____

Are you or your spouse registered members of a political party?

75. Yourself   76. Your spouse

(1)_____   Not a member   (1)_____
(2)_____   Member of Democratic Party   (2)_____
(3)_____   Member of Republican Party   (3)_____
(4)_____   Member of another party   (4)_____
(0)_____   Not Applicable   (0)_____
(BL)_____   N. K.   (BL)_____

Do you and your spouse generally vote in political elections - local, state or national?

77. Yourself   78. Your spouse

(1)_____   Never vote   (1)_____
(2)_____   Rarely vote   (2)_____
(3)_____   Occasionally vote   (3)_____
(4)_____   Generally vote   (4)_____
(5)_____   Always vote   (5)_____
(0)_____   Not Applicable   (0)_____
(BL)_____   N. K.   (BL)_____

79. Have you or members of your family ever used any of the local community health and welfare services or facilities listed below?

(1)_____ Used none of them
(2)_____ Used one of them infrequently
(3)_____ Used one of them a number of times
(4)_____ Used two of them, both infrequently
(5)_____ Used two of them, at least one of them a number
           of times
(6)_____ Used three or more of them
(BL)_____ N.K.

Please check as many of the services you have used

_____ Counseling and mental health
_____ Group work, social and recreational
_____ Clinics and hospital outpatient
_____ Public assistance
_____ Vocational training and rehabilitation
_____ Public housing
_____ Homemaker
_____ Day care for children
_____ Placement and foster homes
_____ Nursing homes for the elderly
_____ Social rehabilitation services for people with special
       problems and needs
_____ Correctional (parole, probation, etc.)
_____ Others, please indicate_____

        We are most grateful to you for giving us time to
pose the many questions and note your opinions on subjects
under study. We wish to assure you again that the information you provided will be treated confidentially.

DO NOT FILL IN (FOR RESEARCH CODER ONLY)
80. Index of Social Position of Family

(1)_____
(2)_____
(3)_____
(4)_____
(5)_____
(6)_____
(7)_____
(8)_____
(9)_____
(0)_____   Not applicable
(BL)_____   N. K.

V. 4. Reliability and Validity

Although the Community Functioning Scale has gone through
a number of time consuming stages of development, it has only been
given a limited field test, and data on reliability and validity are
still in short supply. A reliability test-retest was carried out with
a group of 50 respondents, and an inter-community comparison of
scale scores, obtained from random samples of interviewees, was
examined for first evidence on scale validity.

The test-retest method is one of the most conclusive means
of establishing the reliability or consistency over time of opinions
held by respondents. Its value as a reliability index is limited by
the problem of finding subjects willing to take the test twice. The
idea of repeated administration of the same instrument is generally
abandoned precisely because "guinea pigs" willing to promote social
methodology--in contradistinction to people who are ready to contribute their views as a means of building knowledge--are not thought
to abound. The problem can undoubtedly be overcome by motivating
potential respondents with better incentives than "a chance to advance
methodology, " namely, material rewards. But the additional expense involved is usually sufficient reason for the investigator to
seek other ways to test reliability.

This investigator chose the path of well-known compromise,
using college students who hopefully are motivated to contribute
their services because they can be persuaded by the "appeal to
science" approach and, alternatively, are likely to cooperate because of the pressures they feel are being exerted by their instruc-
tors. Two classes of students in the Rutgers Graduate School of
Social Work were used as subjects. The classes were of unequal
size, numbering 36 and 24, respectively. The first class was
made up of entering students who had had a limited amount of class
work and no field experience. The second group was composed of
students who had completed one year of work and whose method of
specialization was community organization.

The first group was thought to be more nearly like the

typical respondent asked to take the community functioning schedule, for they had had no training in identifying and assessing community problems, skills which might conceivably be correlated with the stability of attitudes on the subject. This group of students differed, however, from the rank and file of potential respondents in level of education (they were graduate students) and interest in the subject of community needs and problems. The second group had completed three-fourths of their course work and two-thirds of their field work as professionals in training at a community organization agency. The first group was asked to complete the schedules by describing the situation prevailing in their home communities. The second group faced the task of referring to the communities in which they were completing their second semester of field work.

While response patterns of neither group could be viewed as being representative of a community population, they were thought to reveal, when compared with each other, the extent to which knowledge of the subject would tend to influence the stability of attitudes. Differences between beginning and advanced students, it was believed, would permit inferences about possible differences between the student population tested here and community residents included in studies but not in the reliability test.

The approach to the test-retest experiment was as follows: the students were asked to participate in a little study, aimed at comparing the prevalence of need for services in various New Jersey communities. A week later they were approached again with the request to complete the schedule a second time, and the purpose of the repeated administration of the questionnaire was revealed to them.

It was assumed that the passing of a week reduces the likelihood that the respondent will recall exactly how he answered the questions on the first test. Further postponement in taking the retest, it is believed, may invalidate the test-retest idea because changes in the community situation may bring about a change in opinions registered. As it turned out, the first group was administered the second test ten days later because of a change in class

schedule. Most members of group 2 took the second test a week
after the first, but four took it two to three weeks later because
of absences.

In view of the fact that one student or another could not be
reached both times, the sample size was reduced to 31 in group 1
and 19 in group 2, leaving a total of 50 sets of usable questionnaires.
Each set is being compared in relation to changes from one administration to the next in terms of the following alternatives of change
on the five point scale:

(1) Respondent checked the same answer both times.

(2) Respondent checked a different answer one scale
    step removed.

(3) Respondent checked a different answer two or more
    scale steps removed. This includes a check of one
    of the four alternatives of service needs (1-4) and
    the other a check of "I know nothing about the sub-
    ject" (5).

The answer to the question of differences in reliability rates
due to respondent's knowledge of subject was given by almost identical rates (63. 5% and 63. 3%) for groups 1 and 2 on "identical response" patterns. This finding made it possible to combine samples
from the first and second test for the further analysis of the consistency of responses.

The mean item reliability (covering 41 schedule items[16])
was 63. 41% with a standard deviation of 6. 87. That is to say, the
average percentage for "no change" responses was 63, but the range
was 80% to 50% from the most to the least reliable item, with
about two-thirds of the items showing a range between 57% and 70%.
The mean percentage for one point changes (either upward or downward) was 30. 68. This left a residual mean percentage of 5. 91
for items registering shifts of more than one scale point or shifts
from a substantive response to a "don't know" answer, or the re-
verse.

When the test-retest analysis is extended to individuals
rather than items, we obtain a mean of 63. 3% with a standard
deviation of 18. 9%. This indicates that the average (mean)

respondent was consistent from one administration of the test to another on nearly two-thirds of the items. The range of response patterns extended from 100% (respondent was consistent on every item) to 27% (respondent was consistent on only about a fourth of the items). Two-thirds of the respondents, as shown by the standard deviation, were consistent on 82% to 44% of the items. For those respondents who changed their scale position one or more points from the first to the second test, the up-and-down movement was reasonably well balanced. The mean upward movement was 15.2% and the mean downward shift 16.2%; in other words, slightly more of the items were scored lower than were scored higher the second time the questionnaire was filled out.

This test-retest reliability is only marginally satisfactory. The reliability ratio, however, can be improved considerably by simplifying the data analysis in a manner which reduces the substantive four point scale (responses 1 to 4) to a dichotomy. This can be done after analyzing the nature of the distribution and determining the optimal cut-off point. Dichotomizing responses in terms of high or low, or those advocating change versus those not advocating it--whichever is statistically most useful--is likely to boost reliability substantially. The present reliability study did not permit this type of analysis because the schedule was completed by respondents who were addressing themselves to different communities and this did not allow for an overall meaningful grouping of responses.

Instrument validity is an infinitely more complex issue than reliability. In the case of the Community Functioning Scale it denotes a correspondence between scale scores and the actual beliefs of community members regarding the adequacy of services and resources to meet need in their community. The tapping of these beliefs was the express purpose for constructing the Community Functioning scale. The most direct way of determining the validity of scale results would be to compare with the results of another, independent measure of community attitudes. This writer, however, is not aware of the existence of such a measure and undoubtedly would have refrained from developing the present tool had another, roughly comparable one been available.

The validity question could be approached by taking a second tack. It could be assumed that people's beliefs are highly correlated with actual conditions and that, therefore, known differences in conditions ought to correspond to measured scale differences. This assumption would seem to be reasonably defensible providing the populations that are being measured are roughly comparable. The reservation put forth in the last sentence rests on the contention that different populations, one native-born and the other new immigrants, or one lower class and the other middle class, would not necessarily react in a similar fashion to given social structures.

The first validity test of the Community Functioning Scale undertook to compare random samples of respondents from two New Jersey communities, New Brunswick and Newark, where populations are approximately 40,000 and 400,000, respectively. Despite size differences, both cities are characterized by a high rate of unemployment, [17] sub-standard housing, [18] low median family income, [19] a high ratio of nonwhite minority groups, [20] and foreign-born residents. [21] On these and other socio-economic indices both cities present a picture of social deprivation and urban decay, and both have experienced racial riots. The problem is more severe in Newark as most of the indices show; the difference, while due to many factors, is at least partly a function of size. The much greater magnitude of the difficulties--racial ghettoes, blighted housing, unemployed who are unable to find jobs, abandoned cars in the streets, etc.--gives the city of Newark an air of despair which is less prevalent in New Brunswick. Because of geographic location and population size, the latter city retains some suburban features which, in the minds of American urbanites, tend to be associated with the good life.

In the light of the situation described above two hypotheses are formulated for testing the validity of the Community Functioning Scale:

(1) The state of social deprivation in both communities is

reflected in the views of the population and results in an overwhelm-
ing expression of attitudes strongly favoring changes in provisions
for services, resources, and opportunities.

(2) The perceived differentials in social and economic
characteristics between Newark and New Brunswick will result
in a stronger endorsement by Newark residents of the need for
changes in service provisions.

Newark data on community functioning were gathered from
a sample of 315 housewives who were part of a larger study on
the longitudinal social functioning of young families. [22] This sample
represented an 89% response of the 352 families originally selected
as a probability sample, [23] those who remained with the research
project to the end. The New Brunswick data comprised 69 heads
of households, two-thirds of them women, drawn randomly as a
one percent random sample of households listed in the city direc-
tory. The attrition rate, due to refusals and the inability of interviewers to find people at home, was about 40%.

The mean rate at which respondents favored changes in the
provisions for services (response alternatives 2, 3, or 4[24]) was
83.5% in Newark and 75.2% in New Brunswick. The respective
mean percentages for primary provisions were 86.8 and 80.23.
For secondary provisions they were 77.9% and 64.6%, respectively.
A comparison of areas for the two cities revealed the distribution
shown on the next page.

The results of the comparison give unequivocal support to
the two hypotheses. In both communities more than three-fourths
of the respondents favored changes in service provisions. Newark
citizens were stronger advocates of change in all areas, although
in one, housing, the difference was too miniscule to be cited in
support of the hypothesis. [25] Striking differences between the two
communities are apparent in provisions for social participation and
recreation and basic socialization, which reflect the absence or in-
accessibility of parks and playgrounds as well as sub-standard
public schools in the city of Newark.

There are enough shortcomings in size and selection pro-

	Newark Percent endorsing change	New Brunswick Percent endorsing change
PRIMARY PROVISIONS		
Income, Employment and Social Security	84. 2	75. 1
Housing	88. 0	87. 9
Basic Socialization	91. 7	71. 0
Health	83. 2	75. 0
Social Adjustment	89. 5	86. 1
SECONDARY PROVISIONS*		
Social Control	83. 2	80. 1
Social Participation and Recreation	92. 8	68. 6
Secondary Socialization	74. 0	59. 7
Provisions for Derived Instrumental Needs	66. 9	53. 1

*The two areas of Social Acceptance and Mobility and Cultural and Religious Expression are excluded from this comparison because they were not contained in the schedule administered in Newark.

cedures of the two samples to recommend caution in the acceptance of the findings on validity. This writer would argue, nonetheless, that this first test, while not conclusive, constitutes overcoming the first major hurdle on that most difficult and studiously avoided validity tract. Further experimentation in reliability and validity testing is the principal mandate to the future user of the Community Functioning Scale.

V. 5. <u>Measurement of Community Functioning - A Postscript</u>

The assessment of community functioning emerges as a rather
anemic effort when compared to the measuring of family functioning,
a seemingly strange situation since it is obvious that the community
is so much more complex a system. From a common sense point
of view it would seem that the respective measurement endeavors
would reflect the complexities of the areas for which they were
designed, and yet precisely the opposite turns out to be the case.
A rather involved technique was devised for measuring the small
and relatively simple social system called family, while an uncom-
plicated method of measurement was prepared for the extremely
complex structure known as community. The answer to this para-
dox lies in the following observation: A simple system allows itself to be studied in depth whereas a complicated one defies all
but gargantuan efforts at comprehensive and thorough evaluation.
Does this statement imply then that the more unsophisticated effort
reported here is actually of questionable utility? This writer believes that the measurement of community functioning by assessing
attitudes toward services, resources, and opportunities serves a
distinct purpose for it contributes significantly to the fields of community planning and organization. It may, on the other hand, be of
lesser importance to the many other disciplines associated with
community study and practice.

It is well to remember that the complexity of the community
system stems from the fact that it encompasses a vast number of
sub-systems, themselves differing enormously in size, tenure, and
structure. Many of these, such as the business and industrial system, the health system, the housing system, and the educational
system, fall within the purview of distinct and separate disciplines
which require special expertise for their study. Any measurement
endeavor which seeks to investigate the effectiveness of these sub-
systems would necessarily take a multi-discipline form. The
greatest problem and also the special challenge in such an undertaking would be to tie specialized inquiries together into an integrated

whole. At the present underdeveloped state of cross-discipline research in the social and behavioral sciences, the notion of intensively studying community functioning is doubtless premature and clearly beyond the mandate this writer has set for himself.

A more modest and, at this point, less utopian approach to the study of community functioning is suggested by the study of social indicators. These indicators are measures designed to reflect the nature and changing character of social situations and processes. In the words of Raymond A. Bauer, social indicators "enable us to assess where we stand and are going with respect to our values and goals, and to evaluate specific programs and determine their impact."[26] An impressive volume by Eleanor B. Sheldon and Wilbert E. Moore[27] deals with social indicators and the study of social changes. While the authors are mainly concerned with monitoring change by analyzing trends in populations, stratification, the family, the economy, religion, politics, and a host of other institutions, they make clear that their purpose is not program evaluation but that it is "heavily weighted toward the scholarly, or analytic, side of the balance between theoretical and practical concerns focusing on large scale structural change."[28] Bauer, by contrast, stresses the use of indicators to improve the state of the nation and achieve national goals.

Whichever purpose suits the researcher, it is obvious that the social indicator movement has great potential for community analysis. It holds promise for developing criteria to judge performance in various areas of human endeavor, and at some stage it could combine these criteria to constitute performance indicators of complex systems such as the community. Work on this is just beginning; to this point it is more in the nature of theoretical treatises or case studies and models rather than actual instruments of measurement.

While acknowledging the fact that our own attempt to measure community functioning falls far short of the goals of cross-discipline community research or those of the social indicators approach, it is necessary to stress some of the advantages of the method de-

veloped here.   It should be remembered, first of all, that the community functioning scale is designed primarily for the use of the
social work and social welfare practitioner, and that the chief concern of that field of practice is the consumer.   Given these foci,
the objective has been to develop an index which sensitively and
comprehensively reflects the state of community health and well-
being.   It is obviously impossible to mount evaluative studies of
every community system which is potentially relevant for the welfare of the population.   As an alternative this writer chose to study
the attitudes of the consumers of services, assessing the opinions
which were expressed on their adequacy or inadequacy and the con-
sequent need or lack of it for services, facilities, and resources.

Some respondents have no knowledge about the quality of
community resources.   This may be seen as a drawback to this
method of evaluation, but the questionnaire has sought to guard
against this by providing the option of a "don't know" response.
It may be contended that an individual might lack good judgment
regarding the quality of services, but the cogency of this argument
is open to doubt.   As a consumer, or a member of a primary
group of consumers, there is nothing irrelevant in the way he responds to services or to the lack of services.   If he does not have
knowledge about what is ultimately best for him or his family,
friends, and neighbors, it is the community's responsibility to en-
lighten him with expert knowledge, if such is indeed available.
The chances are that on many, if not most, issues the attitudes
of those being served--or not served--is one of the most important
sets of data which can be gathered for the purpose of judging the
quality of services and resources.

In the final analysis the worth of the community functioning
scale is to be judged (aside from its reliability and validity which
are methodological considerations) by the degree of sensitivity with
which it mirrors a social situation which must concern planners
and practitioners alike.   The present instrument is organized as
to levels of need and the priorities of areas of service, so that
the subject of community resources can be dealt with from these
two perspectives.

There remains the long range issue of demonstrating the utility of the community functioning scale, not only as a valid index of attitudes but as a true indicator of the community's social situation. And with this statement our chain of arguments has come full circle, for in order to prove that community attitudes are indeed good indicators of the interrelationship between actual needs and available resources we need to be able to apply the aforementioned techniques of measurement--multi-discipline or social indicator--for which the present community functioning scale is but a second alternative.

VI. FAMILY AND COMMUNITY - SOME HYPOTHESES

To summarize the effort reported in this manual, we must
return to the introductory thesis which held that family and community functioning are reciprocally relevant concepts.   According to social systems theory, to which this volume owes a great deal, this
interrelationship of concept is inherent in the fact that the family
is a system which generally operates within that of the community.
Given this observation a number of others follows: the family is
dependent upon the community, and its own social functioning is
partly determined by the nature of community functioning.   Communities, in turn, are strongly influenced by the structure, attitudes, and behavior of the families in their midst, which constitute
one of the most basic social systems they encompass.   Substantial
changes in either system are bound to have effects upon the other.

It is the latter thesis that has substantial implications for
social work policy and practice.   Although the time is probably
past when an agency was concerned exclusively with its client and
oblivious to the needs and requirements of those persons and systems with which he maintained contact (this approach was particularly
characteristic of traditional psychotherapy), the present American
welfare structure still reveals a predominantly narrow and primary
client-focused pattern of service.

This is not the place to enumerate the many reasons for
this individualized and fragmented social welfare picture.   It is
sufficient to say that efforts at integration would be aided substantially by methods which would permit the assessment of needs and
the exploration of problems of client systems which are reciprocally
related, such as family and community.   Neither family treatment
nor community planning and organization can be practiced effectively
without an awareness of and reference to each other.   Service to
families is heavily dependent upon the resources and facilities

furnished by the community, while strategies of community organization are guided in part by the nature of family life within the community's boundaries.   Changes in one are bound to have far-reaching implications for the other.   Widespread unemployment, for example, will affect local consumption patterns, taxes, job training
programs, rehabilitation and financial assistance resources, and a
host of other factors.   An increase in family disorganization,
whether due to delinquency, drug abuse, out-of-wedlock births, or
economic strains, has a great impact on the community's welfare
budget, its social services and correctional system, and perhaps
on the manner in which priorities for the future will be ordered.

The evaluative techniques presented in this manual enable
both the service planner and practitioner to seek answers to important practice and policy related questions.   A few examples of
such questions are stated below in the form of hypotheses based
upon the conceptual frameworks presented in Charts I and III:

(1)   The performance level of the community integrative
system, i. e. , the provision of resources and services to meet
the needs of the population, is directly related to the family's
instrumental functioning.   Stated differently, it can be said that
the family's ability to maintain itself as a physical system depends
to a large measure on the kind of provisions the community has
established for the welfare of its citizens.   This hypothesis would
direct planners and social service practitioners toward an examina-
tion of the temporal relationship between the quality of services and
the instrumental aspects of family functioning.   Verification of the
hypothesis would counteract a widespread tendency to view problematic behavior in the economic, health, and housing areas as inherent
in the life style of certain kinds of families. [1]   A two-pronged approach should be used to test the foregoing hypothesis: a compara-
tive study of communities that differ in their integrative service
level, holding social class and ethnic characteristics constant; a
longitudinal study in which changes over time in services are correlated with changes in instrumental family functioning.

(2)   Changes over time in the community's integrative serv-

ice system are related to changes in the family's expressive functioning. This hypothesis actually postulates a chain reaction, in which
services first affect instrumental family behavior and that, in turn,
influences the nature of functioning in the intra- and extra-familial
relationship areas. [2] It is asserted, then, that integrative community
services affect expressive family functioning indirectly by their impact on instrumental family behavior.

The relationship over time between expressive and instrumental family functioning is not well researched. In one study, where
a clinical and predominantly lower-class population was investigated,
the inference was drawn that problems in the expressive areas pre-
cede malfunctioning in instrumental behavior. [3] Results of another
study on the interrelationship of family problems "contradicted the
assumption that economic problems of families are related to personal ones and also the clinical assumption that interpersonal problems in the marital and parental roles are closely related."[4] On
the other hand, Blood and Wolfe found marital satisfaction positively
related to social status[5] while this writer found a strong direct cor-
relation between social status and family functioning among young
urban families. [6] A further study of a clinical population also found
that practical difficulties, interpersonal conflict, and personal de-
fects and maladjustment were significantly interrelated. [7] None of
these studies examined the relationships among types of functioning
from the perspective of change over time, however.

Those who are interested in planning community strategies
which attempt to strengthen family life will be interested in verify-
ing or disproving the above hypothesis, for support of the hypothesis
would suggest that high priority be given to the augmenting of integrative services at the community level.

(3) The degree of importance which the community has assigned to the goal of autonomy (which covers provisions for derived
instrumental needs and social control functions) tends to affect the
prevalence of social and economic dependency among families.
Lower-class families, very young families, and old families with
limited earning power are likely to manifest a community dependency

which is not present in the more affluent segments of the population.
The former groups rely more on local shopping and transportation
facilities as well as police protection (residents of low income areas
are the most frequent subjects of street violence) than does the
more mobile middle class.   The verification of this hypothesis has
substantial consequences for community planning.   An increase in
socio-economically dependent population groups--whether this be
due to migration or changes in the economic situation--would require
a corresponding shift in resources and services to meet the needs
of the groups most affected.

(4)   The family's viability, i. e. , its capacity to confront
problems and survive under adverse conditions, is directly affected
by the community's primary provisions of those services which meet
basic survival needs.   This hypothesis would necessarily need to be
tested at a time of crisis, whether this be an economic or social
upheaval or a natural disaster.   Given a number of communities
with similar populations, those with more adequate provisions to
assist in the areas of income, employment, health, and social adjustment are most likely to arrest the process of family breakup
and disorganization.   The significance of this hypothesis lies in
the realm of prevention, a promising but underdeveloped area in
the helping professions.

(5)   The success of broadly gauged intervention programs
designed to help improve the social functioning of deprived families
is directly related to the quality of all the relevant community resources.   This hypothesis is in need of testing by reviewing the
outcome of such projects in relation to the services, resources,
and facilities which exist at the community level.   At least one
study, whose goal was the prevention of family organization, gave
evidence that poor resources were an inhibiting factor in the attainment of action objectives. [8]   Since so many anti-poverty projects
mushroomed in the wake of the 1964 declaration of War on Poverty,
this thesis of the interrelationship between the quality of appropriate
services and an improvement in the social functioning of the poor
would be of great interest but it has received little systematic

attention. Project after project has been conducted under some
organization's favorite slogan or banner: the poor need more job
training or better health services or cheaper transportation or more
participation in decision making. There followed inevitably a demonstration project designed to meet one or the other of the projected
and probably accurately assessed needs. But the results, if known--
and more often than not they did not become known--were generally
no change or insignificant change in the social functioning of the
poor. These projects have paid scant attention to the many interrelated problems and needs of the target populations and to the
failures of these endeavors--which invariably involved community
resources as a whole--to deal with the issues in the order of importance.

The latter hypothesis touches upon a key consideration in the
mobilizing of any effort aimed at modifying the social conditions of
individuals and groups. Medicine and psychiatrists have long paid
lip service to the needs of the total man and the total family but
family medicine and family psychiatry have only gradually emerged
and grown, indicating that an awareness of the problem is not necessarily tantamount to institutional change. The other social helping
professions, particularly social work, have borrowed heavily from
social science theory which stresses the systems approach, but it
is much more emphasized in professional writings than in professional practice.

One of the preconditions for translating a seemingly promising approach into institutional forms is the availability of tools.
Such tools would permit the practitioner to begin with an assessment
of conditions and delineation of problems affecting the total individual,
group, or system. After all, the planning and rendering of services
must necessarily be firmly based on such a prior assessment. The
two instruments which we have presented here to evaluate the social
functioning of families and communities do not cover--let alone ex-
haust--the need for such research implements in this area. Although one hopes the two scales will prove useful to the researcher
and practitioner, they are above all an illustration of that which

remains to be done and that which can be done in shifting professional action from tradition, insight, and practice wisdom to objective knowledge and tested theory.

Chapter Notes

CHAPTER II

1. Catherine S. Chilman (editor), <u>Approaches to the Measurement</u>
    <u>of Family Change</u>, Washington, D. C. : U. S. Department of
    Health, Education, and Welfare, Welfare Administration,
    June 1966, p. 4.

2. For a full discussion of this subject see Harry C. Bredemeier,
    "The Socially Handicapped and the Agencies: A Market
    Analysis, " in Frank Riessman, Jerome Cohen, and Arthur
    Pearl (editors), <u>Mental Health of the Poor: New Treatment</u>
    <u>Approaches for Low Income People</u>, New York: Free Press
    of Glencoe, 1964, pp. 88-109.

CHAPTER III

1. Werner W. Boehm, <u>Objectives of the Social Work Curriculum</u>
    <u>of the Future</u>, VoL 1, p. 46; also Ruth M. Butler, An
    <u>Orientation to Knowledge in Human Growth and Behavior</u>,
    <u>VoL VI, p. 24; A Project Report of the Curriculum Study</u>,
    Council on Social Work Education, New York, 1959.

2. Ideas in the present paragraph are a partial reiteration of
    thoughts formulated by the author in an earlier article.
    See Ludwig L. Geismar, "The Concept of Community Func-
    tioning in Social Work: Preliminary Formulations, " <u>Journal</u>
    <u>of Jewish Communal Service</u>, VoL 42, No. 3, Spring 1966,
    pp. 227-233.

3. Blaine E. Mercer, <u>The American Community</u>, Random House,
    N. Y. , 1956, p. 8. Structure is defined by Mercer as the
    arrangement of individuals in relationships defined and con-
    trolled by patterns of standards, values, customs or be-
    havioral norms. Definitions of the concepts function and
    functioning were based on the writings of Radcliffe-Brown.
    See A. R. Radcliffe-Brown, <u>Structure and Function in</u>
    <u>Primitive Society</u>, New York: The Free Press, 1965,
    pp. 178-187 (book was first published in Great Britain in
    1952).

4. Roland L. Warren, "Toward a Non-Utopian Normative Model
    of the Community, " <u>American Sociological Review</u>, VoL 35,
    No. 2, April 1970, pp. 219-228. Warren does not include
    integration but cites "broad distribution of community

decision-making power" as a third goal. This value was
seen as too narrowly focused to merit inclusion as a
separate dimension applicable to family and community
systems.

5. Ibid., p. 223.

6. Homans argues forcefully "that the general explanatory prin-
ciples even of sociology are not sociological as the func-
tionists would have them be, but psychological, propositions
about the behavior of men, not about the behavior of societies. " George C. Homans, "Bringing Men Back In, " American Sociological Review, Vol. 29, No. 6, December 1964,
pp. 809-818.

7. Conrad M. Arensberg and Solon T. Kimball, "Community
Study: Retrospect and Prospect, " American Journal of
Sociology, Vol. 73, No. 6, May 1968, pp. 691-705.

8. Ibid., p. 691.

CHAPTER IV

1. For a well articulated formulation of this position see Nathan W.
Ackerman, The Psychodynamics of Family Life, Diagnosis
and Treatment of Family Relationships, New York: Basic
Books, Inc. , 1958.

2. Leonard S. Kogan and Ann W. Shyne, "The C. S. S. Movement
Scale: A Methodological Review, " in Catherine S. Chilman,
op. cit. , pp. 12-19, p. 15.

3. Ibid.

4. L. L. Geismar and Beverly Ayres, Measuring Family Func-
tioning, A Manual on a Method for Evaluating the Social
Functioning of Disorganized Families, St. Paul, Minn. :
Family Centered Project. 1960.

5. See several articles on the subject in Part I, Introduction of
Norman W. Bell and Ezra Vogel, A Modern Introduction
to the Family, Glencoe, Illinois: The Free Press, 1960,
pp. 37-97. See also Part III, "The Family in Its Societal
Setting, " in Harold T. Christensen (editor), Handbook of
Marriage and the Family, Chicago: Rand, McNally and
Company, 1964, pp. 401-500.

6. Bell and Vogel, op. cit. , p. 19.

7. For reviews of the structural-functional approach to family
study see Jesse Pitts, "The Structural-Functional Approach, "
in Harold T. Christensen, op. cit. , pp. 51-124; Jennie
McIntyre, "The Structure-Functional Approach to Family

Study, " in F. Ivan Nye and Felix M. Berardo, Emerging Conceptual Frameworks in Family Analysis, New York: The Macmillan Company, 1966, pp. 52-77.

8. William J. Goode, "The Sociology of the Family, " in Robert K. Merton, Leonard Broom, and Leonard S. Cottrell, Jr. (editors), Sociology Today, New York: Basic Books, Inc. , 1959, pp. 178-196, p. 188.

9. Levy as quoted and interpreted in Jennie McIntyre, op. cit. , pp. 70-71.

10. Kingsley Davis, Human Society, New York: The Macmillan Company, 1948, pp. 394-396.

11. Ian Whitaker, "The Nature and Value of Functionalism in Sociology, " in Don Martindale (editor), Functionalism in the Social Sciences, Philadelphia: The American Academy of Political and Social Science, February, 1965, Monograph 5, pp. 127-143.

12. Edward A. Suchman, Evaluative Research, New York: Russell Sage Foundation, 1967, pp. 32-33.

13. For a discussion on composite vs. simple measures, see Matilda White Riley, Sociological Research I, A Case Approach, New York: Harcourt, Brace and World, Inc. , 1963, pp. 337-338.

14. Edwin J. Thomas and Bruce J. Biddle, "Basic Concepts for Classifying the Phenomena of Role, " in Biddle and Thomas (editors), Role Theory: Concepts and Research, New York: John Wiley and Sons, Inc. , 1966, pp. 23-45.

15. Reproduced with permission of the publisher from L. L. Geismar and Beverly Ayres, Measuring Family Functioning, St. Paul Minn. : Family Centered Project, Greater St. Paul Community Chest and Councils, Inc. , 1960, pp. 91-100. Some revisions have been made by the Neighborhood Improvement Project, New Haven, Conn. , and the Rutgers Family Life Improvement Project, Newark, N. J.

16. Ibid. , pp. 75-90.

17. Ludwig L. Geismar, Ursula Gerhart, and Bruce Lagay in collaboration with Harriet Fink and Isabel Wolock, The Rutgers University Family Life Improvement Project - Final Report, New Brunswick, N. J. : Rutgers University, Graduate School of Social Work, 1970 (Preliminary version, mimeographed).

18. L. L. Geismar and Beverly Ayres, Patterns of Change in Problem Families, St. Paul, Minn. : Family Centered Project, 1959. Gordon E. Brown (editor), The Multi-Problem Dilemma, Metuchen, N. J. : The Scarecrow Press, Inc. , 1968.

19. Ludwig L. Geismar and Jane Krisberg, The Forgotten Neigh-borhood, Metuchen, N. J. : The Scarecrow Press, Inc. , 1967, p. 330. Geismar and Ayres, Patterns of Change in Problem Families, pp. 8-9.

20. Ludwig L. Geismar, "Family Functioning as an Index of Need for Welfare Services," Family Process, Vol. 3, No. 1, March 1964, pp. 99-113. Ludwig L. Geismar, Preventive Intervention in Social Work, Metuchen, N. J. : The Scare-crow Press, Inc. , 1969, pp. 29-36.

21. L. L. Geismar, Michael A. LaSorte, and Beverly Ayres, "Measuring Family Disorganization," Marriage and Family Living, Vol. 24, No. 1, 1962, pp. 52-60.

22. A sub-category factor analysis done with a sample of 555 young urban families yielded five factors composed of variables with loadings ranging from .577 to .838. The factors were tentatively identified as expressive-inter-personal relationships, instrumental functioning, economic functioning, formal associations, and health conditions. Some of the original, theoretical main categories such as family relationships and economic functioning emerged from the principal factor method of analysis intact, while others such as Care and Training of Children were split up among two factors: training and emotional care appeared as a variable on the expressive-interpersonal dimension, while physical care had its highest loading under instrumental functioning.

23. Geismar and Ayres, Measuring Family Functioning, pp. 37-42.

24. Ibid. , p. 21-51.

25. Geismar and Krisberg, The Forgotten Neighborhood, pp. 320-321.

26. David Wallace, "The Chemung County Evaluation of Casework Service to Dependent Multi-Problem Families: Another Prob-lem Outcome," The Social Service Review, Vol. 41, No. 4, December 1967, pp. 379-389. For a more detailed ac-count of the study see David Wallace and Jesse Smith, The Chemung County Research Demonstration with Dependent Multi-Problem Families, New York: The State Charities Aid Association, 1965, pp. 17-49.

27. Matilda White Riley, Sociological Research - I - A Case Ap-proach, New York: Harcourt, Brace, and World, Inc. , 1963, p. 474.

28. Geismar, LaSorte, and Ayres, loc. cit.

29. Geismar, Gerhart, and Lagay, op. cit. , p. 55.

30. Ibid., pp. 29-43.

31. Wallace, loc. cit., pp. 387-388.

32. Geismar, Gerhart, and Lagay, op. cit., pp. 119-124. Also The Rutgers Four Agency Study, comparing three forms of evaluation of client movement during treatment (Manuscript in preparation).

33. John Crane, Louis Reimer, and Susan Poulos, An Experiment in the Development of Welfare Aides, Vancouver, B. C.: Children's Aid Society of Vancouver, British Columbia, Canada, June 1970, p. 27ff. Joel G. Sacks, Panke M. Bradley, and Dorothy Fahs Beck, Clients' Progress Within Five Interviews, New York: Family Service Association of America, 1970, pp. 52-81.

CHAPTER V

1. Meyer Schwartz, "Community Organization," in Harry L. Lurie (editor), Encyclopedia of Social Work, New York: National Association of Social Workers, 1965, pp. 177-190; p. 177.

2. The exceptions were a number of community studies on social and recreational needs and community surveys like the Family Unit Report Study of Community Research Associates in which need assessment was based on a reporting of populations using health and welfare services.

3. For a criticism of the approach and a comparison of the priorities of community leaders and the rank and file, see Ludwig L. Geismar and Bruce W. Lagay, "Planners' and Consumers' Priorities of Social Welfare Needs," Social Work Practice, 1965, New York: Columbia University Press, 1965, pp. 76-95.

4. Roland L. Warren, The Community in America, Chicago, Ill.: Rand McNally and Co., 1963, p. 9.

5. Ibid.

6. Ibid., pp. 9-10.

7. Edward O. Moe, "Consulting with a Community System: A Case Study," Journal of Social Issues, XV, No. 2, 1959, p. 29.

8. Warren, op. cit., p. 49.

9. This is not to say that it cannot be done. The issue is rather that standardized evaluations on many communities would be most difficult because of the need to take account of a large variety of sub-systems.

10. Geismar, Ludwig L., "The Concept of Community Functioning; Preliminary Formulations," loc. cit., p. 231. The term unmet need is redundant; if a need were met it would cease to be a need.

11. Ibid., p. 231.

12. Ibid., pp. 232-233. I am indebted to Professor Albert Comanor of the University of Calgary for the idea expressed here.

13. Leo Nover, Carol T. Pollak, Stephanie G. Robinson, and Melvin Slawik, A Study of the Social Welfare Needs of the New Brunswick Area, New Brunswick, N. J.: Rutgers University, Graduate School of Social Work, May, 1961 (Unpublished MSW Thesis).

14. Geismar and Lagay, "Planners' and Consumers' Priorities of Social Welfare Needs," loc. cit., pp. 76-93.

15. Geismar, Gerhart, and Lagay, op. cit., pp. 135-140.

16. The 42nd item "clean air and water" was added after completion of the reliability study in the wake of some recent community needs studies which revealed the clean air and water question as a high priority issue for action.

17. The Newark estimate was 9.1% for 1967. Source: Jack Chernick, Bernard P. Indik, and George Sternlieb, Newark, New Jersey Population and Labor Force, New Brunswick, N. J.: Institute of Management and Labor Relations, Rutgers University, Dec. 1967, p. XII. The 1960 census lists the New Brunswick rate as 5.6%.

18. Fourteen percent of New Brunswick homes were rated as substandard in 1960. Source: Georgina M. Smith, An Outline of Poverty in Middlesex County, New Brunswick, N. J.: Middlesex County Economic Opportunities Corporation, 1967, p. 16. A third of Newark houses were judged to be dilapidated. Source: Thomas R. Brooks, "Newark," The Atlantic, Vol. 224, No. 2, Aug. 1969, pp. 4-12; p. 8.

19. Seventeen percent of Newark's households reported family incomes of less than $3,000 a year in 1966. Source: Chernick et. al., op. cit., p. XIII. The 1959 rate for New Brunswick was 15.3. Source: Smith, op. cit., p. 16.

20. Negroes were reported to comprise 52% of the population of Newark in 1967. Nearly 10% were of Spanish-speaking origin, mainly Puerto Rican. Source: Chernick, et. al., op. cit., p. XI. The percentage of Negroes and Puerto Ricans in New Brunswick was 37.0 and 12.1, respectively in 1960, and presumed to be much higher near the end of the 1960's when the study was done. Source: Smith, op. cit., pp. 17-18.

21. The 1960 rates for foreign-born were 12% for Newark.
    Source: Georgina Smith, On the Welfare, New Brunswick,
    N. J.: Research Section, Institute of Management and Labor
    Relations, Rutgers University, May 1967, p. 12. The New
    Brunswick rate for 1960 was 14%. Smith, An Outline of
    Poverty in Middlesex County, p. 18.

22. Geismar, Gerhart and Lagay, op. cit.

23. The original sample was drawn from the universe of all young
    mothers under 30 who gave birth to a first child in 1964
    and the first third of 1965. For details see Geismar, Ger-
    hart, and Lagay, op. cit. , pp. 10-28

24. The response alternative excluded from this tally is: services,
    resources, and opportunities are adequate as they are.

25. The reasons for the lack of difference in housing are not en-
    tirely clear. They might be explained by a higher level of
    aspiration in New Brunswick, set by the superior quality of
    housing in surrounding communities.

26. Raymond A. Bauer, "Detection and Anticipation of Impact:
    The Nature of the Task, " in Raymond A. Bauer (editor),
    Social Indicators, Cambridge, Mass. : The M. I. T. Press,
    1967, pp. 1-67; p. 1.

27. Eleanor Bernert Sheldon and Wilbert E. Moore, Indicators of
    Social Change, New York: Russell Sage Foundation, 1968.

28. Ibid. , p. 4.

CHAPTER VI

1. The question of life style vs. social situation as an explana-
   tion of the behavior of the poor was dealt with in Helen I.
   Safa, "The Poor Are Like Everyone Else, Oscar, " Psychology Today, Vol. 4, No. 4, September, 1970, pp. 26-32.

2. We concede that changes in instrumental areas need not be the
   result of change in services but may occur in response to
   other factors. The present hypothesis, however, addresses
   itself specifically to relationships between family and community.

3. Geismar, "Family Functioning as an Index of Need for Welfare
   Services, " loc. cit.

4. Orville G. Brim, Jr. , Roy W. Fairchild, and Edgar F.
   Borgatta, "Relations Between Family Problems, " in
   Marvin B. Sussman, editor, Sourcebook in Marriage
   and the Family, Boston: Houghton Mifflin Company,
   1963, pp. 359-367.

5. Robert O. Blood and Donald M. Wolfe, Husbands and Wives, New York: The Free Press, 1965, pp. 253-255.

6. Geismar, Preventive Intervention in Social Work, pp. 35-40.

7. Jessey Krupinski, Elizabeth Marshall, and Valerie Yule, "Patterns of Marital Problems in Marriage Guidance Clients," Journal of Marriage and the Family, Vol. 32, No. 1, February 1970, pp. 138-143.

8. Geismar, Gerhart, and Lagay, op. cit., pp. 79-93, 141-142.

Bruce, J., 31, 204
tools for research, 200

U. S. Department of Health,
   Education and Welfare, Social
   and Rehabilitation Service, 10;
   Welfare Department, 10
urban middle-class families, 31
Use of Community Resources,
   category of Profile, 31, 40, 48;
   criteria for rating, 69-71

validity of Community Functioning
   Questionnaire, 185, 188-191
validity of evaluating community
   functioning, 162
validity of Family Functioning
   Scale, 137, 139-140
viability and community, 154
Vogel, Ezra, see Bell, Norman
   W.

Wallace, David, 139-140,
   205, 206
Wallace, David and Smith,
   Jessey, 139
Warren, Roland L., 14, 154-
   155, 202, 203, 206
Whitaker, Ian, 26, 204
Wolfe, Donald M. see Blood,
   Robert O.

Yule, Valerie, see Krupinski,
   Jessey

Z family case study, 77-114;
   ratings, 114-128